PEOPLE AT THE BOTTOM

By the same Author

Social Dimensions of Water Supply and Sanitation in Rural Areas
The Changing Munda
Shifting Cultivation in India
Social Change in Village India

About the Author

Professor Sachchidananda, currently Director of the Sulabh Institute of Development Studies, has been a pioneer in the field of anthropological studies in Bihar. He was educated in the Patna University and the School of Oriental and African Studies, University of London. Founder of the Post-graduate Department of Anthropology at Ranchi, he was later Director of the Bihar Tribal Research Institute, Ranchi and of the A.N. Sinha Institute of Social Studies at Patna. He was also the Vice-Chancellor of Ranchi University. His wide ranging research interests cover culture change in tribal areas, shifting cultivation, social dimensions of agricultural development, Harijan educated elite, women's rights, educational problems of the disadvantaged sections of the population, voluntary action in tribal areas and socio-cultural dimensions of development. He has contributed a large number of papers to research journals in India and abroad and published twenty-three books in Sociology and Anthropology. He has also edited the four volume 'Profile of Indian Tribes (1995)'. A past President of the Anthropology Section of Indian Science Congress, he is also the recepient of R.P. Chanda and S.C. Roy Medals for distinguished work in Anthropology from the Asiatic Society of Bengal.

PEOPLE AT THE BOTTOM

A Portrait of the Scavengers

SACHCHIDANANDA

Director

Sulabh Institute of Development Studies, Patna

Former Director

A.N. Sinha Institute of Social Studies

and

Former Vice-Chancellor

Ranchi University

CONCEPT PUBLISHING COMPANY, NEW DELHI-110059

ISBN 81-7022-906-5

First Published 2001

Published and Printed by
Ashok Kumar Mittal
Concept Publishing Company
A/15-16, Commercial Block, Mohan Garden
NEW DELHI-110059

Phones : 5648039, 5649024
Fax : 091-11-5648053
E-mail : publishing@conceptpub.com

PREFACE

Scavengers in Bihar are at the lowest rung of society. They constitute the people at the bottom. They are the real Antyaja as conceived by Mahatma Gandhi. Although the scavengers are with us since beginning of civilization, there are no detailed studies of their living and working conditions, their troubles and tribulations, their hopes and frustrations. The main purpose of the study is to get some idea of the living and working conditions of different scavenger castes in Bihar and to bring out the impact of different welfare programmes for their liberation and rehabilitation. An attempt has also been made to study the implications of the changing scenario from the gender and human right perspectives. Efforts to bring the scavengers from the margin to the mainstream of the society and ultimately to empower them has also been assessed in terms of the success achieved.

The study covered nearly 2500 households in urban and rural areas in Bihar. Intensive field work was done for four months by a number of investigators, employing the usual tools of data collection such as observation, schedules, group interviews and case studies. Secondary data was also used whenever necessary.

It is hoped that the study will give a rounded picture of scavengers and their problems in the vortex of change. Towards the end of the study some suggestions have been made for improving their condition speedily in the near future.

I would like to thank all members of the research team for the labour they put in in spite of the problems of field work. I am deeply obliged to the Sulabh International Social Service Organisation for supporting this research.

I am grateful to Shri Ashok Mittal for seeing the book through the press.

SACHCHIDANANDA
Director
Sulabh Institute of Development Studies, Patna

CONTENTS

CONTENTS

1

SCAVENGERS IN INDIAN SOCIETY

Conceptual Background

It is a paradox of modern times that the spirit of the age is in favour of equality though practice denies it almost everywhere. The more one is attached to the ideology of equality the more oppressive the reality becomes. All efforts of the State are aimed at reducing the inequalities and yet, in some spheres, if not in all, the inequalities are increasing (Sachchidananda, 1994).

There is a tendency in South East Asia to view equality as an "economic" problem. The plans embody western economic concepts and theories and are stated in financial and fiscal terms; even public discussion about planning is largely restricted to "economic" issues. The effect is to exclude from close and continuous scrutiny the institutions and attitudes responsible for social inequality (Myrdal, G., 1968). But in contrast, socially created inequality consists of the different privileges which some men enjoy to the prejudice of others, combined with the continuation of old values and old habits of mind.

Clearly the egalitarian society remains a dream. All human societies from simplest to complex have some form of social inequality. In particular power, prestige and profession are unequally distributed between individuals and social groups. Some of these societies have a very complicated social structure with a highly developed class consciousness in its members (Fuchs, S., 1981). Since the Indian social system is unique and not found in other parts of the world, it inherits the principle of inequality formally recognized as governing all social relations combined with the scale of hierarchy set up on well-known rules. There are two essential characteristics of social hierarchy: first, status is determined by principles independent of the distribution of authority; and second, the idiom in which higher or lower status is expressed is the idiom of purity (Dumont, 1970).

In other parts of Asia, Europe, America and Africa etc., although there is some system of social stratification, they are quite different in nature and based on economic, social and ethnic considerations. Examples of such socially stigmatized groups are the blacksmiths of Arabia, Somaliland and in certain animal breeding societies of East Africa, the pygmy tribes of Central and Southern Africa, a section of the Arioi Society in Tahiti and the South American Maku. In the past centuries the Jews of medieval Europe, the shepherds in Germany, later the Negroes of North America, the Blacks and coloured in South Africa, the aborigines of Australia, the Yetas of Japan, and in the modern times the Jews in Nazi Germany, and to some extent the present "guest workers" in Europe.

Degrading Pursuit

Hindu society in traditional India was divided into five main strata: four varnas, and the fifth group the outcaste, whose members were untouchables. Each caste is sub-divided into jati or sub-caste. Jati is an occupational group ranged in terms of ritual purity. The occupations of the first two *varnas* are clearly stated to be priesthood, administrative and military duties respectively. Below them the Vaishyas, in modern usage, were mainly merchants, and finally the Shudras were the producers. At the bottom are the untouchables who are regarded as unclean, base and impure, a status which affects all their social relationships. They must perform unclean and degrading tasks such as disposal of dead animals and scavenging. They must be segregated from members of the caste system and live on the outskirts of villages or in their own settlements.

The post-Vedic period witnessed the growth and consolidation of power due to the presense of hereditary groups in a hierarchy with Brahmins at the top and the untouchables at the bottom. These untouchables are called by different names such as "Harijans" (a glorified term, coined by Narsimha Mehta and adopted and popularised by Mahatma Gandhi), "Exterior Castes" (J.H. Hutton), "Depressed Classes" and "Dalit".

The Dalit, too, had traditional occupations but with a distant difference. By and large their occupations were least desirable and defiling (Srivastava, B.N., 1997). Apart from regional and local occupational variations the Dalit had mainly two main categories of profession, namely, leather processing and cleaning or sweeping. A caste working as remover of nightsoil and the cleaner of latrines belongs to a well defined group in the Indian social structure. All such workers in India are today covered under the general term "Scavenger". For this occupational group there are various names and titles in use in different parts of the country but the better known terms are 'The Mehtar' and its Mohammedan counterpart 'The Halalkhor'.

Cleaning or sweeping involved sweeping of streets, drains and sewers; removal of human and animal excreta; raising of pigs, etc. Since toilets in most cities were not provided with flush, the sweepers had to carry buckets of human faeces on his or her head. Their jobs are not only degrading, polluting and tedious, but they are also poorly paid. To eat the left-over of the another person's plate is considered highly degrading. It is a common practice among the scavengers to collect one or two chapatis from the houses they serve. Although this is a part of their customary rights and wages, it amounts almost to begging. This practice of collecting food is gradually disappearing from big cities, but it is still very much prevalent in small towns and villages.

Origin of Scavenging

Ancient books do not mention any caste like the scavengers or removers of nightsoil among the traditional occupations nor do they mention of any caste exclusively relegated to this profession. Even to this day scavenging as a profession does not exist in most of the rural areas.

The institutionalisation of 'sweeping and scavenging' as a profession seems to be of recent origin. There is a reference in

Kautilya's Arthashastra that during Maurya period defecation in an open space in the towns was prohibited but there is no mention about the disposal of nightsoil by scavengers. The old scriptures, however, throw some light on the system of scavenging. Dr. Bindeshwar Pathak (1991) writes in his 'Road to Freedom' that "according to the contents of the scriptures and other literatures, scavenging, especially the disposal of nightsoil by a particular caste or castes of Indian society, has been in existence since the beginning of civilisation with the emergence of towns. One of the fifteen duties for slaves enumerated in the Naradiya Samhita was to dispose of human excreta. In Vajasaneyi Samhita the Chandals and Paulkosa have been referred to as slaves for the disposal of nightsoil. It is said that only after the advent of the Muslims in India "sweeping and scavenging" seems to have taken the form of a formal profession. It is said that the system of bucket privies was designed and constructed by Muslims for their women in purdah. Those who were made captives, were forced to clean latrines, bucket privies and throw off the nightsoil at distant places. These captives, when freed, were not accepted by the society and they formed a separate caste and continued the work of scavenging. During the British period with the setting up of army cantonments and municipalities, a large number of people were perhaps required to provide this service on a regular basis.

Descent from Valmiki

According to a myth, current among the older generation of the Bhangis, they are descendants of Valmiki Rishi, the first Sanskrit poet and famous author of the Hindu epic the Ramayana. Their supposed connection with Valmiki rests on occupational and not on racial identity. Valmiki's story, as it prevails among the *Bhangis*, represents him as a low caste person making a living as a robber.

Anthropological View

When Aryans came here as conquerors, they retained with themselves the religious and military functions of the social order.

So as time rolled by, they held the functions of princes and nobles and became large holders of land. The conquered people were kept in subjugation. They performed the lowest task which was scavenging only. Later on some variations in the features of the members of the groups emerged partly by the fact that their entry as servants into high class families facilities illicit connection with superior class and partly that tribe habitually recruits itself by admission of outcaste from superior tribes (Crook, 1896).

Sociological Perspective

Not much has been written on scavenging by sociologists about its inception, existence, desirability and epistemology, although many sociologists used the terms social inequality and social stratification to illustrate the situation combined with hierarchy of social groups that has been replaced by a hierarchy of individuals with a common identity, like interests and similar life-styles. Talcott Parsons (1951) has brought to light the universal rationale of hierarchy. He says that "occupational stratification is an inevitable part of all human societies, therefore, it will result in ranking of individuals in terms of common values and thus it is desirable for the system to function" as is the occupation of scavenging. Parsons does so because he combines the intellectualism of Durkheim (recognizing that action is dominated by representations or ideas) and the pragmatism of Max Weber (confronting, beyond the problem of the representation of the world, that of action in the world as represented). Contrary to the functionalist view, the Marxist regard social stratification as divisive rather than an integrative structure. They see it as a mechanism where by some exploit others rather than a means of furthering collective goals. In tune with the radicals Wallace and Wallace (1989) go to the extent to say that "the Indian caste system is one of the most notoriously successful, longest running fraud in history".

Social Functions

The names of scavenging castes suggest that they are a functional community recruited from many different racial and social groups. It is very likely that people belonging to the lowest strata were compelled to take on this profession especially in the urban areas due to economic necessity.

Stephen Fuchs (1981) has pointed out that "the endogamous sub-sections of this lowest of all low-castes, are not without a certain social gradation. Within the scavenging caste some sections are superior to others, and the social status is determined according to the origin of the section, claiming a former higher rank, or according to the type of work a particular section is doing. The lowest place is generally occupied by those sections which carry nightsoil. The highest sections have given up scavenging entirely, and have adopted other occupations, such a leather work, weaving or farming.

Among these lowest scavenging sections which remove nightsoil there is still a distinction; those who serve in private houses consider themselves higher than those who clean public latrines. It should not be forgotton that this type of work has to be carried out in urban environment and in villages where the women are not permitted to leave the house, even where it is for a call of nature. Each of these sub-sections has its own rules and regulations as to what work is permitted and where the line is to be drawn. Some do not touch nightsoil, but do all other scavenging work in the villages, including the removal of dead animals and garbage.

Conversion and Excommunication

This theory emerges from the tradition current in Hindu society, according to which breach of established social norms and usage was a social crime. Anyone who violated these approved social laws was guilty and was declared an outcaste. This means that the position of the excommunicated goes down and they are treated as untouchables and were also prohibited from following their traditional occupation. Now they were with no means of livelihood. Without it they might starve. It would be natural in these circumstances for these outcastes to agree to give to others their services as sweepers (Shyamlal, 1992). In Hindu society this happened from early times. This process is still going on. As a consequence, there always existed a floating population consisting of persons formerly belonging to different castes.

Being Bhangi

Another view is that the term *Bhangi* originally derived from Sanskrit root Bhang (Hemp) and Bhangi meaning "Hemp Addict". Crook (1896) in support of this derivation advances the 'Buria custom of calling their leader Bhangi or Hemp addict as a title of honour'. The Bhangis are to be regarded as a group of hemp drinkers. A much wider connotation of the term *Bhangi* has been put forward by an eminent economist the late Professor D.R. Gadgil (1952). According to him "Bhangis are castes traditionally confined to the business of removing nightsoil. They are on this account considered among the most degraded in Hindu society. Moving out of the caste occupation is, therefore, extremely difficult for them".

The scavenging castes which are known by different names in different states like Bhangi, Balmiki, Chuhra, Mehtar, Mazhabi, Lalbegi, Halalkhor, etc. in northern India; Hari, Hela, Dom, Senei, etc. in eastern India; Mukhiyar, Thoti, Chachati, Pakay, Relli, etc. in southern India; and Mehtar, Bhangi, Halalkhor, Ghasi, Olangna, Zadmalli, Barvashia, Metariya, Jamphoda, Mela, etc. in western and central India, also made efforts to get united and have a common name. In 1911 Census, some of them started returning as Adi Dharmi, Adi Dravida, Adi Karnataka and Adi Andhra. Hutton, in 1931, estimated the population of various scavenging castes as 20 lakhs in undivided India. After independence, the census in 1961 estimated their population to be 8.2 lakhs. The number of scavengers who were engaged in the removal of nightsoil was 3,86,725 which can be projected as 6.18 lakhs for 1981. The Task Force constituted by the Planning Commission had estimated the number of scavengers in respect of scheduled castes for the year 1989 at 40 lakhs, out of which 3,33,779 were in urban areas and 67,220 in rural areas. In the urban areas 2,06,612 were male and 1,27,167 female. In the rural areas, 53,335 were estimated to be male and 13,865 female. This rural and urban distribution of scavenging caste shows that 83 per cent scavengers are located in urban areas and 17 per cent in the rural areas.

In Bihar according to an estimation of the Planning Commission (1989), the number of scavengers is 22,400, out of which 10 per cent reside in rural areas.

Prior to the estimation of the Planning Commission (1989), the census of Bihar in its report of 1961 had estimated the total number of persons engaged in the occupation of scavenging as 17,057, out of which 10,480 were males and 6,577 females. Out of the male category, 2,461 resided in rural areas whereas 8,019 in urban areas. In the female category 1,220 resided in rural areas and 5,357 in urban areas.

There is a general misconception that all scavengers are scheduled castes and are, therefore, entitled to the benefits provided for the scheduled castes in the Constitution. Persons professing religion other than Hindu, Sikh, or Buddhist like Christianity, Islam or Tribal cannot be scheduled caste and are thus not entitled to the benefits. The perfect example can be the Halalkhor and Lalbegi who are Muslims.

However, the members of those occupational groups which were not included in the list of scheduled castes, have now been included in the Central list of Backward Classes in accordance with the Supreme Court judgement of November 1992 and are now entitled to all the benefits which are admissible to the Backward Classes by the Central and State Governments.

Scavengers in Bihar Society

Family

Nuclear family system is a predominant feature of the scavenger community, although joint families are also found.

The nuclear family is composed of parents and unmarried children only, whereas, the joint family consists of parents with married children living together. In some cases separated or widow daughter is also found in the joint family. To some extent a scavenger family based on intimacy and emotional attachment in fact masks a system of exploitation of wives by husbands and children by parents by promoting occupational continuity.

Socialisation

The birth of a child is an important occasion in the scavenger community. The ceremonial *Chhathi* is performed on the sixth day of the child's birth. Relatives and other friends are invited for a ceremonial gathering. Liquor and meat are the foremost items to be served. Exchange of gifts takes place and everybody blesses the new born.

The next ceremony is *Mundan* in which the first hair-cut is performed. As in *Chhathi*, relatives and friends are invited for a dinner. A change has come in some recent years in the attitude of the barber who performs the hair-cut. Previously, the scavengers had to look for a barber from a far-off place for this ceremony, as the local barber did not oblige. But in recent years the local barber has started rendering his services for the ceremony. But the local barber serves them only on the occasion of 'Mundan'. The logic behind this courtesy is the fee he gets for the job.

Like other caste Hindus, the scavengers also learn the culture of their society through the process of socialisation. Primary factors for socialisation are their family, neighbour, the community and peer group. The urban and rural set-up, other than their community, is the secondary factor.

Sanskritisation and westernisation are also playing a major role in the process of socialisation of the scavengers. Both in rural and urban areas the scavengers are eager that their children adopt the local caste culture. But as Harold G. Gould (1961) observes "often the motive force behind Sanskritisation is not cultural imitation, but an expression of challenge and revolt against the socio-economic deprivation".

Certain customs traditionally associated with the high castes which not only continue but are gaining ground among what is usually termed the westernised elite have also influenced the scavengers. Western clothing worn by younger generation, especially on festivals and social gatherings, along with adoption of certain values regarding literacy and trade union activity can be cited as examples. In case of scavengers, adoption of both 'western' and 'sanskritised' styles is primarily an indication of the standardisation or breakdown of separate "little traditions" associated with urbanisation.

Marriage

Scavengers, like other high and low caste Hindus, perform a series of rites and rituals in connection with marriage. Each marriage ceremony is linked up with a chain of rituals performed in minute details.

Initially, the father of the girl looks for a suitable boy. Once a boy is located he informs his caste elders and takes their consent. The local caste leaders who work as intermediaries visit the bridegroom's house where they are given a red carpet welcome. The hospitality includes liquor and meat along with gifts. After the approval of the middlemen the parents along with relatives of the bridegroom visit the bride's house to meet her, and thus, the marriage is fixed. Dowry in cash and kind is foremost requirement in a scavenger's marriage and the amount depends on the earning of the bridegroom and his family stutus.

The scavengers are strictly an endogamous group with only a few cases of inter-caste marriage. Previously it was considered to be a matter of grave concern, but at present the rigidity has been relaxed to a great extent. This change in attitude is an outcome of value assimilation of the scavengers with the caste Hindu. Incidence of love marriage in their community no more produces shock, as it is confined within the same caste.

Besides caste endogamy, scavengers' marriages are also regulated by *gotra* or clan exogamy. No person is allowed to marry within his own gotra. Such a marriage is tabooed.

Divorce and Remarriage

Divorce and remarriage are common among the scavengers. A wife, who does not get along well with her husband or there are specific grievances either on her part or that of her husband, may go for divorce. The simplest way of divorce among the scavengers is when a wife goes and lives in her parental house and refuses to return to her husband's house even when invited. Such a refusal indicates her desire to settle elsewhere. Divorse can be obtained formally or informally.

Remarriage after divorce is also common among the scavengers and is socially sanctioned. Remarriage after spouse's death is also allowed. Old widowers and widows do not remarry.

There is sanction for polygamous marriage among the scavengers, especially among the Halalkhor and Lalbegi, as they are Muslims. Among the reasons for polygamous marriage are the advantage of taking up more work and earning more with more wives. In recent years due to gradual process of Sanskritisation this community is also trying to adopt monogamous norms.

Marriage is conducted by the priest. But these priests are not allowed to conduct the marriage or other social rituals of the caste Hindus. Scavengers have a separate priest who covers a fixed area and no other priest is allowed in that area for scavengers' service. In the hierarchy of Brahmins these purohits are assigned the lowest rank. For the followers of Islam, no such distinction is in practice. The Halalkhor and Lalbegi avail the services of the same Mulla for the marriage who serves other sections of the Muslims.

Religion

The religious beliefs and practices of the scavengers are not very different from those of the Hindus. They worship the same gods and goddesses of upper caste Hindus despite the fact that they are not allowed to enter the temples particularly in rural areas. The scavengers of Bihar worship the Goddess *Shakti*. Above all, the educated scavengers now put great emphasis on Hindu customs. Many of them have stopped eating beef and lay great emphasis on vegetarianism. Especially the Rajasthani scavengers of Ranchi are more religious than their local counterparts and are often seen performing religious rituals in their own community.

The Halalkhor and Lalbegi scavengers are the followers of Islam. They have easy access to the place of worship and are free to visit other higher caste people (Ashrafs) of their own religion. Halalkhor and Lalbegi are free to attend the religious social gatherings but still in Islam also the scavengers have some stigma attached to them regarding their unclean occupation being converts from untouchable caste Hindus, as assumed by the high ranking strata in Muslim community. However, Islamisation as a process of status mobility within the Islamic social structural framework has replaced vertical mobility in caste by increased trends towards horizontal consolidation of the power of castes.

Hindu scavengers are cremated after their death while the Halalkhor are buried.

Religious Sects

In Bihar there are some scavengers who call them self Kabir-Panthi. They admire Kabir's teaching and in personal life try to practise it. It is a 'conversionist sect', voluntary in nature, demanding total commitment from its followers and emphasizing its separateness from the mainstream religious ideology.

Other than Kabir-Panthis, there are some scavengers in the Tirhut and Mithila divisions of Bihar who admire Supan Bhagat, a contemporary of Lord Krishna in Hindu mythology and regard him as their cultural hero.

Social Status

Scavengers have been regarded as untouchables. The Indian Constitution clearly forbids the practice of untouchability and has prescribed safeguards for them, which either specifically or in general terms seek to promote their educational and economic interests and to remove the social disabilities and discrimination they suffer. On the level of principle the problem is solved. But neither equal status nor economic advance has been yet achieved by them.

The problem of untouchability is not only a problem of caste Hindus but the hierarchy of different castes based on the notion of pollution and purity is also present among the untouchables. In Bihar the scavengers do not take food and water from Dhobi, Dusadh, Pasi and Teli and consider them more polluting than themselves. However, there is a potential bond among the scavengers and other scheduled caste people, no matter what their relative status is, they are all low in caste in relation to members of higher castes. All are somehow or other economically dependent upon the members of the higher castes.

Apparently, caste Hindus refer to a scavenger as untouchable. They do not take food or water from him. Their touch will pollute food, water and utensils used for cooking or eating. The scavengers are regarded as defiling especially because of their degrading traditional occupation of removing nightsoil and because of their eating carrion, beef and meat of other dead animals. Despite the fact that their services have been accepted as highly valuable, often necessary for the survival of society, the poor people have been treated like contagious disease, calling for disdainful distance and minimal social contact. They have been debarred from entering Hindu temples and from offering prayers in the places of worship. Because of their social degradation, scavengers have been compelled to a life of social disadvantage. They have been forced to accept their social degradation, discrimination and disadvantaged position as part of their fate, despite the great importance of the work they do for the health and hygiene of the people whom they serve.

Scavengers are mostly concentrated in urban areas and live in segregated bastis in the most crowded parts of the cities and towns. The scavengers occupation is looked down upon with such detestation that scavengers living in the heart of the town are physically segregated and socially isolated. They remain untouchable, unapproachable and are not allowed in the house except for scavenging.

Their social, economic and cultural marginality in the society is reflected and reinforced by their place in the village settlement pattern. Although, low in caste they are fuctionally related to higher castes. They depend upon the members of the higher castes for their livelihood. Some of the marriage and death rituals cannot be completed without the participation of the scavenger caste. For example, the winnowing fan which is used for offering prayer to the Sun god in Chhat and the basket which is used in different rituals in a caste Hindu marriage are socially acknowledged as their creation. Above all, the Mukhagni (the fire which ignites the funeral pyre) is provided by none other than a Dom.

The scavenger occupies an isolated position in the ceremonial life. Although they follow the customs and rituals of the members of higher castes, they worship gods and goddesses separately in their own houses or locality. Similarly, they do not join the members of the higher castes in any ritual. As traditional workers for all higher castes, they receive food and other domestic things at important festivals, such as Holi, Diwali, Chhat etc., but they do not celebrate these festivals on equal terms with the members of other higher castes. Culturally, they are outside the Hindu Sanskritic Great Tradition and are part of the pre-literate local Little Tradition.

Their social status can be summarized as follows:

- Scavengers constitute an underprivileged social group treated as 'Impute' and consequently ritually avoided.
- They are treated as inferior and often regarded as less than human. They live on the fringe of society, often excluded from social contact, although their services are accepted as highly valuable.
- They are socially ostracised because of their ritual impurity and for certain peculiar objectionable habits and ritual polluting profession.
- They are backward, and often oppressed, not because of their alleged racial, social and cultural inferiority, but simply because they have been assigned the lowest of the low status in social hierarchy.
- As outcastes and rejects of the Indian society, scavengers have suffered human indignities throughout the ages.
- They have been treated like dreaded contagious disease calling for a disdainfull distance and the most minimal social contact.
- Because of their social degradation, scavengers have been compelled to live as socially disadvantaged persons condemned to accepting their social degradation, discrimination and disadvantaged position as part of their

fate.

— Besides social backwardness, scavengers are economically backward too. Most scavenger families, therefore, live in poverty because of structural factors as low family income on account of being engaged in low paying occupations, and personal factors as their large family size and male memebrs' indulgence in smoking, drinking and gambling.
— Most scavengers are illiterate and thus educationally backward. In spite of the facilities for their free education, children are not sent to schools in most cases, and female education is not considered to be an important issue.
— The economic and educational backwardness has deprived many scavenger families from taking advantage of the privileges meant for the welfare of the dispossessed.
— Politically too, scavengers are poorly organised as compared to other castes.
— While in recent years there has been some change in the traditional occupational structure of the scavengers, a large majority of them are still given to traditional hereditary occupations.

Economic Status

Scavengers are economically tied to the city especially to the members of higher castes as traditional workers. The scavengers' traditional work is sweeping and removing garbage in the city. Most of these scavengers are attached with the Municipal Corporation/ Nigam as permanent or temporary workers. The rest are working in big nursing homes, private companies or other establishments where their services are required. The condition of urban scavengers is somewhat better because they get their salary at the end of the month.

Apart from these, there are scavengers who earn their livelihood by serving individual households. This category is economically worst affected.

The rural scene is different. In rural areas, the village is divided among different scavenger families for cleaning of toilets. Each rural scavenger family has been serving a certain number of households

(*Jajmans*) from generation to generation. In principle, the *jajmani* system makes use of hereditary personal relationships to express the division of labour.

The *Jajman* compensates his scavenger through periodic payments in cash/kind. Scavengers also receive gifts such as clothing, food, raw materials, etc. on Holi, Diwali, Chhat and other important occasions like birth, upnayan, mundan, marriage and death.

It is an unwritten law that if a scavenger wants to move out of the village or from the area of operation, he would have to find a substitute in his place. If he wants to sell his customary right, he could do so to another family of his own caste. The sale is only effective on the condition that in that particular area no other scavenger has any claim and also that the person who bought it is satisfied. The price would be fixed according to the income of the area. After the price is fixed the transfer is performed in Registry Office or in front of local Mukhiya in a legal manner.

This fixed occupational area is also used as *Patta* at the time of need. Money can be lent from other scavenger by leasing him the area for a certain period of time. When the loan is repaid the owner regains his occupancy right over the area. This is a formally sanctioned system among the rural scavengers in Bihar.

Apart from traditional occupation, outside employment in non-traditional occupations is a recent phenomenon among the scavengers in Bihar. Very few had the opportunity to join the Government sector jobs other than traditional occupation, except some Rajasthani scavengers of Ranchi who have become small entrepreneurs.

Occupational Mobility

The social distance between the occupationally mobile Bhangis and the rest of the society is very much there. Although a few have achieved occupational status due to their absorption in government job on respectable posts in recent years, the attitude of the caste Hindus towards them is not friendly. Their integration with the upper castes is not an easy thing. Occupation mobility does not guarantee their integration into the larger society. While their aspirations for economic betterment have been fulfilled to some extent, the achieved status does not result in their acceptance as equals. They often find themselves isolated and alone. However, occupationally mobile Bhangis do have some social interaction with the upper castes, but it remains confined to a limited sphere. Their commensality, marriage and most other social relations are confined to their own caste. Their awareness for change of occupations is evident from a study conducted by Sulabh International Patna (1996), which reveals that out of the total, only 32 per cent have diverted from their traditional occupation and most of them are in private sector job. This figure shows the situation of the state capital where undoubtably the literacy and occupational mobility rates are higher than in other parts of the state and thus can be attributed as an urban phenomenon, not a universal process. Job reservation policy of the government has brought no relief and others do not accept the special treatment for the scheduled castes in the same spirit. Most of the educated Bhangis nurture feelings of hurt and grievance. This in turn arouses dissatisfaction and resentment towards the larger society.

Occupational mobility has also led to other castes and tribes entering this profession. The erstwhile castes and tribes who used to consider scavenger as impure and scavenging as degrading profession have started joining this profession. Tribals have joined Tata Group of Companies at Jamshedpur and Coal India Limited at Dhanbad as scavengers. However, they do not identify themselves with the scavenger caste.

In rural areas due to gradual conversion of dry privies into pour flush toilets and Sulab Shauchalaya, some scavengers have taken up bamboo work in north Bihar as it remunerates them throughout the year.

Trade Unionism

Trade union is a common phenomenon among the scavengers in the urban set-up. Scavengers are making efficient use of trade unionism because few castes are prepared to challenge their monopoly of a low status, yet socially indispensable, occupation. Scavengers working in Municipal Corporation or Nigam find these trade unions as a platform to bargain their demands which are mainly: (1) payment of salary on time; (2) payment of overtime rate for work done during free time; (3) scavengers working as daily worker on daily wages should be made permanent; (4) availability of mechanical tool for work; (5) shoes to protect their feet; (6) annual paid leave; (7) sanitation should be given the status of skilled occupation; (8) adequate housing facility; (9) money raised from fines for absenteeism should be spent on free education, books and medical treatment for their children; (10) end of redtapism in the Municipal office; (11) service to the dependants of those who die during service; (12) when a worker retires, preference for temporary or permanent work should be given to members of his family; (13) retirement benefits, etc.

The Municipal Corporation is tired of the scavengers' ever increasing demands as it feels that they have already got too much of the local body's scarce resources. In reality many of the demands related to the implementation of provisions have already been granted to them but only on paper. Scavengers themselves are not united and are members of different trade unions. Some of the union leaders go against the interests of the workers to gain their own personal and political ends. Scavengers themselves also feel preplexed about leadership and thus they are wary of trade union leaders from outside. Their profession and caste has also hurt their cause.

In rural areas the caste association works as trade union to look after the cause of the scavengers. The main reason for dispute in the rural area is the interference of the outsider scavenger in areas fixed for other scavengers. In certain incidents of interference a meeting is called upon and the matter is placed before the leaders of caste association for their opinion which later becomes a judgement. These associations are regular bodies and have office-bearers from the same caste.

Political Aspirations

Political means are another avenue whereby lower castes have striven to raise their economic and social status. The dilemma for the lower castes has been whether to work along with the upper castes or separate from them under the banner of scheduled caste parties. Economic demands by deprived groups have political consequences. Reservation quota for scheduled castes in political representation and in jobs has reinforced caste consciousness in politics.

There was no homogeneity in the past among all the polluting castes. Nor is it there even today. In fact, pre-existing differentiations among various deprived castes have been reinforced by the modern political processes. Now, interest groups have started exerting their pressure through political means.

During the last decade, there has been some political reform in this community. The political emergence of the so-called 'Third Force' at the state and national level has given them a sense of participation in the political affairs. Apart from Ambedkar, Gandhi and Phule who happen to be their all-time favourties, leaders like Buta Singh and Bhola Ram Toofani also provide them a political ego, as they themselves belong to the scavenging caste. Along with vibrant political ideologies, they have given them a sense of identity. The radical jargons and insight also generated many changes in their society and demands like separate electorate and provision for separate reserved constituency are coming up.

Now many political opinion leaders can be found in this community. They are assertive and conscious of their rights. In participation in voting, party mobilisation and in contesting election, their caste identity is no more a taboo. The most important characteristic of this community is their habit of en-bloc voting which sometimes creates caste hostility with the caste Hindus.

Scavengers use vrious tactics for reducing their marginality. The awareness of exploitation and deprivation has led to politicization and unionization by the group to assert themselves. Political resources being a prerequisite for success in pursuing economic interests, representation in political bodies is attempted, agitations launched and associations are formed. However, the caste-based reservation of seats in central and state legislatures, politicization and unionization have encouraged and intensified consciousness of caste identity. This reservation ensures access to education, employment and political representation.

2

REVIEW OF STUDIES

Scavengers as a community have not received adequate attention from sociologists and anthropologists. There are brief casual references in Risley, Crooke, Thurston, Russell and Hiralal about scavenger castes in different parts of the country. Very few ethnographic studies or research papers on them are available although they are found in all the states in the country. Some monographs on scavenger communities outside Bihar have been reviewed. Two reports on training and rehabilitation of scavengers and some papers dealing with some aspects of the Bhangis have been discussed.

1. THE BHANGI—A SWEEPER CASTE: ITS SOCIO-ECONOMIC PORTRAIT: By *Shyam Lal*, Popular Prakashan, Bombay, 1992

The main object of the study is to undertake a study of the Bhangi caste to collect detailed data in view of the following reasons :

— Past researches on the Bhangi caste reflect casual and apathetic approach even in scholarly and academic studies.
— Bhangi problem is a sociological problem.
— The significance of the problem may be seen in the light of the progress reported in some researches carried out among the scheduled castes of Rajasthan.

Methodology

The study is confined to the city of Jodhpur. It is based upon depth interviews, case studies and observation of 400 families living in 21 Bhangi bustees. The respondents have been chosen on the basis of purposive sampling from educationally advanced families as also from social and political workers through schedules and interviews.

Findings

People belonging to one *Mohalla* have their own Panchayat. The main function of such Mohalla Panchayat, known as *Mohalla* Ma-Baap, mainly centres around social welfare of the Mohalla. It also meets to settle cases of divorce, family partition and other minor social and cultural disputes. In addition to this another council also called Caste Panchayat exists in the area under study.

There is no preference for junior levirate among the Bhangis. If an outsider wishes to marry the widow he must secure permission and compensate her husband's family. Elopement is another way by which a widow marries the man of her choice. There is no evidence of sororate, wherein a deceased wife is replaced by her sister.

Relationships between parents and children are cordial particularly in the childhood. The mother in the family is generally closer to the children and has a strong affectionate bond with them than the father. Majority of the fathers neither spend good deal of time with their children nor check bad habits such as smoking, gambling, vagrancy and use of vulgar language. When children grow up, it is not unusual to see them at loggerheads with their parents.

Bhangis indulge in reckless expenditure in social and religious ceremonies. They adhere to their customs. A money-lender tides over their difficulties whenever they approach him for help. When they are unable to return the loan, they resort to dishonest and unscrupulous means. This behaviour compels them to mortgage the house and ornaments and other belongings.

A marked rise in the standard of living is noticeable in the families of the *Bhangis*. Apart from increased average expenditure on food, they spend more on education and clothing. Expenses on mutton, edible oil, dress and other items are also quite high.

The Bhangi worship a host of deified ghosts or spirits and Mata (Goddess) Lalbeg, Ram, Vishnu, Chandana besides those followed by majority of the Hindus. They also respect different religious sects. Democratic influence is quite visible in these sects from the fact that many of the preceptors were drawn from low castes. These preceptors emphasised equality amongst all castes and communities and that is why the Bhangi follow different sects. The Guru also occupies a significant position in the religious life of a Bhangi. Bhangis believe that it is only with Guru's help that one can get salvation and attain human life without going through all the *Chourasi Lakh Yonis* or series of rebirths. Guru is vested with powers of curing disease with medicines and spells.

2. SCAVENGER IN INDIAN SOCIETY : By *Rama Sharma*, M.D. Publications Pvt. Ltd., New Delhi, 1995

The study attempts to explore as to how the concept of stigmatized identity relates to the Bhangis and their attempts to shed that identity; the manifestation of their identity in their struggles on political, economic and social fronts, the recession of their marginality with the politicization process and the forces reinforcing their stigmatized identity leading to breakdown.

Methodology

The universe of the study is Delhi. Anthropological techniques and methods are used in association with what is called the 'holistic depiction', a methodological entity. The intensive techniques are participant observation, general 'open ended' interviews, informal conversation, meeting people, participation in events, keeping diaries, etc.

Findings

Private scavenging is known by various names in Delhi and is also called *Jajmani* by *Bhangis*. Bhangis are very emphatic regarding their customary rights, even if the right extends to toilet work in private households. *Bhangis* would not like to forgo these rights as it gives them an assured source of livelihood and extra income if some members of the family are in scavenging employment of the municipality, despite the fact that the Bhangi women's being employed in this work adversely affects their family and the interests of the children.

The large majority of Bhangi men and women are still in the traditional caste occupation, although Bhangis of younger generation are resentful of the association of their caste with the occupation of sweeping and scavenging. Those in this age group who are still in this occupation are determined that their children will be educated and shall not be sweepers or scavengers. Those who have taken up other occupations have certainty paved the way for their children's occupational mobility.

The Balmiki identity has provided a framework within which members of the Bhangi caste have attained group identity. Bhangis now have their own temples, lay priests and their own way of celebrating festivals. This sets them apart from their other Hindu neighbours, a separation symbolized by the Balmiki temple in every Bhangi neighbourhood. These religious symbols have generated in them segregation instead of integration with the rest of the society.

Some Bhangis have made successful political careers mainly through reserved seats in local municipal bodies and Metropolitan Council. Once they win, they enter the world of privileges, amenities and influence which is a complete departure from their previous low social status. Such Bhangi elite suffer a dual isolation. They are no longer at the level of their community, rather they tend to cut themselves away from their broader ethnic base and sometimes assume an exploitative role *vis-a-vis* other members of their caste. At the same time they are not accepted fully by the upper caste fellow politicians.

Trade union has become a platform for the Bhangis to bargain their demands. In Delhi the strikes of scavengers have become frequent. The support of different political parties to the union of scavengers has provided them moral support but at the same time this also leads to fragmentation of the union.

3. REVERSIBLE SEX ROLES : A SPECIAL CASE OF BENARAS SWEEPERS: By *Mary Searle Chatterjee*, Pergamon Press, Oxford, England, 1981

Objectives

The main objectives of the study is to find out how sweepers organize their lives and what it is that holds them together as a group distinct from the larger society and methods they use to try and improve the conditions in which they live and work. The study also probes the relationship between men and women and the varying forms that these take in different areas of their social organization.

Methodology

The universe for the study is Benaras City. With the help of purposive sampling method a sample of 1,400 persons was selected and interviewed with the help of interview schedule. Intensive case and community studies were also conducted along with participant observation.

Findings

Sweepers in Benaras are now an urban community. They do not send remittances to the villages though rural links are an important part of their networks. Girls come and go as brides to and from the rural areas. Changes in the nature of their occupation as well as geographical mobility are leading to the fusion of endogamous sections previously having a hypergamous relationship.

Conditions are altering but the pattern of sweeper life is not changing greatly though the style of behaviour is in some ways moving closer to that of the larger society. Kinship is still of great importance. Social mobility is low and there is rigid segregation of the group from other social castes and classes.

Government policies attempting to raise sweepers from their traditional subservience have met with little success. Occupational mobility is minimal and literacy levels are low though they show signs of improvement. It is only in political attitudes that evidence of change is seen.

Sweepers are beginning to bargain not because of government policies but because they are better placed than other low castes in that their labour is now in high demand and few castes are prepared to challenge their monopoly of a ritually polluting yet indispensable task. Sweepers are working in the spirit of trade union and their revolutionary potential along with other low castes must not be underestimated.

Leadership, however, is in the hands of men. The Sanitation Workers Union, thc only association in which sweepers are active, is organized only by men though women sometimes attend meetings and participate in processions. All the persons referred to as leaders of the community are male. Literacy is confined only to males.

Social attitudes allow women to delegate thc work of child care to husbands or others so that women may do outside work, whether paid or otherwise, in fact enabling them to have a variety of occupations and locale, it does not allow them the same freedom for purpose of recreation or leadership. Husbands look after the child while women go out to sweep or to purchase food, they do not go out for social visits. Men, on the other hand, have both freedoms.

Nature of a women's economic contribution has important consequences for various aspects of status. Independence brings many gains, physical and psychological. Sweeper women are free to divorce a husband whom they find intolerable and free also to marry again. They can as a last resort survive without any financial contribution from their husbands but the fact that a family budget is usually based on a double income means that a woman with children and without a husband does, in fact, suffer a considerable drop in living standards even though she is not destitute or totally dependent as the high caste women may be.

Sweeper women are by no means inarticulate and they speak up in gatherings. They are involved in all that happens in the locality and they share the same concerns and interests as men. They are in no way isolated from other women. There are no corporate female activities or associations.

4. **RESTORATION OF HUMAN DIGNITY** : By *Bakshi D. Sinha, P.S.K. Menon* and *Arun K. Ghosh* (Council for Social Development), Arnold Publication, New Delhi, 1994

This is an evaluation of the existing social and economic status of the scavenger community after assessing the implementation strategy followed by the Government (both Central and State) with regard to various development policies and programmes for their upliftment as well as to suggest appropriate strategy for upgradation of this community.

Methodology

The study was taken up in four states, *viz.*, Andhra Pradesh, Maharashtra, Orissa and Rajasthan. From each state two towns were selected and from each town, a sample of 100 households (50 scavenger and 50 non-scavenger SC families) was selected on the basis of proportionate probability sample. Community case studies in different scavenger localities were conducted to assess the living conditions of the scavenger community.

The authors have made the following important points :

No serious attempt has been made to tackle the problem of scavenger in particular, though efforts seem to have been initiated to mitigate the hardship of the scheduled castes in general.

The information available at various levels with regard to the benefits accrued to scavengers, as one of the most vulnerable sections among schedule castes is sketchy and unimpressive.

The permanent solution for liberation of scavengers and their rehabilitation is complete conversion of dry latrines into pour flush latrines.

The prime reason for slow progress of conversion is not availability of funds but absence of effective coordination at crucial levels of implementation.

The scavengers are placed better than the non-scavenger scheduled castes in terms of income, expenditure, saving and possession of movable assets.

A significant number of non-scavengers are opting for the job of sweepers in municipal bodies. The attitude of other caste people towards them has changed for the better.

Social distance between the scavengers and non-scavenger scheduled caste population is narrowing.

There is practically no difference between the scavengers and non-scanvengers in the overall percentage of educational attainment.

The percentage of families with five members is larger among scavengers than that among non-scavengers. The scavengers have taken loan for improvement in housing facilities apart from improvement in socio-economic conditions by launching self-employment. This is a positive trend which needs to be sustained and encouraged.

Voluntary organizations have a crucial role to play not only in the implementation of various development programmes but also in creating social awareness for self-development among the scavengers. A standing committee may be constituted in the local body with due representation of voluntary organization and local association. This standing committee which should review, monitor and conduct concurrent evaluation of the development programme.

5. **MANUAL SCAVENGING IN INDIA: A DISGRACE TO THE COUNTRY** : By *B.N. Srivastava*, Concept Publishing Company, New Delhi, 1997

An attempt has been made to trace the origin of scavengers in India, their social and economic status, caste organisations, cultural heritage and territorial distribution apart from focusing on the initiatives taken by Central and State Government and prominent non-Government organisations.

Methodology

The study is based on secondary data. Different concerned

Government reports have been extensively used.

Findings

In order to escape the curse of untouchability, a large number of sweepers, mostly in northern India, have abandoned Hindu religion and embraced Islam, Christianity and Sikh religions. But this change of religion has not brought any significant change in their occupation or social status though these religions reject the caste system and express equality of all men.

The sweepers and scavengers of northern India go by various names. The most common name is that of '*Mehtar*' which really means 'prince' or leader. The term '*Bhangi*' is derived from the Sanskrit word Bhang meaning hemp: it seems to be an allusion to their drinking habits. Another name for them is Halalkhor, one who eats what is lawful, or one whose earnings are legitimate.

Besides the emergence of Sulabh International Social Service Organisation as the most effective and dynamic voluntary organisation contributing to the liberation of scavengers, some other voluntary organisations have done pioneering work in this field. The most prominent amongst them are the Harijan Sevak Sangh; Safai Vidyalaya, Ahmedabad; and the Gandhi Smarak Nidhi, Pune.

Other than Central Rural Sanitation Programme which was started in 1986-87, there are a number of programmes under which sanitary latrines are being constructed in the rural areas like Indira Awas Yojana, Employment Guarantee Programme for Rural Landless (RLEGP) and National Employment Programme.

The Ministry of Welfare which is responsible for the rehabilitation of scavengers is implementing the scheme in isolation, without knowing whether the scavengers have been liberated from manual scavenging or are still engaged in this obnoxious sytem. There is no co-ordination between the Ministries of Welfare and Urban Development either at the Central or State level.

Whenever cash compensation is not possible, or the local bodies cannot offer employment under them, the affected scavengers must be taken in other services. Most of the scavengers would be prepared to forgo their customary rights if employed in the municipalities.

In places where there are no scavenging castes, such a cess should be levied and the scavenging services municipalised. This cess should be so adjusted that scavenging services may become almost self-supporting.

6. **ROAD TO FREEDOM :** By *Bindeswar Pathak,* Motilal Banarsidas Publishers, New Delhi, 1991

This is a sociological investigation of the liberation of scavengers through low cost sanitation. The main objectives of the study were the following :

(a) The extent of adoption of various schemes of Sulabh Shauchalaya.
(b) The role of formal organization in adoption of the scheme.
(c) The physical and environmental change ushered through the scheme.
(d) The role of variables like sex, education, caste, religion, place of residence, occupation, exposure to media, organisational affiliation in making the scheme popular among the people.
(e) To identify gaps in the study of sociology of urban sanitation and to provide insight for improvement in the pattern of analysis and generalization in this field.
(f) To find out the constraints faced by the adopters of the scheme and to explore the ways for their removal.

Methodology

The study is based on exploratory research design. The universe for the study is Bihar. With the help of purposive sampling a total sample of 600 units was selected from four sub-universes of adopters, non-adopters, liberated scavengers and unliberated scavengers. Further, with the help of four different structured interview schedules data has been collected.

Findings

The scavengers are conscious of the fact that they and their children are illiterate or semi-literate and unskilled. The scavengers regard themselves superior to Dom, Dusadh, Musahar or Chamar. They also recognise the inter-caste difference among themselves.

There has been a change in the attitude and outlook of the other caste people towards scavengers. The traditional sactions are still in operation though the rigidity of the past has been relaxed. The scavengers did not complain of any discriminatory behaviour with their children or family members in school, office and in getting house on rent.

Liberated scavengers are satisfied with the present occupation. There has been marked change in the social position and outlook of the liberated scavengers. They are now conscious that they have given up the dirty job of scavenging and are different from the unliberated scavengers.

The Sulabh Shauchalaya scheme has been effective not only in liberating the scavengers or initiating the process of abolishing the scavenging but also in mobilising public opinion in favour of the programme and has created a stir in the entire Indian society.

The economic and social backwardness of the liberated scavengers has adversely affected the education of their children. They are not attending schools and they are not receiving even primary education. On the one hand, economic backwardness is responsible for the low percentage of literacy in the younger generation and, on the other hand, social backwardness and lack of social consciousness are responsible for the low percentage of children attending schools.

Their opinion regarding Sulabh Shauchalaya scheme is positive. People not only support the scheme but have expressed their desire to implement it and to extend its area of operation. Those who are not covered by the programme are willing to be benefited by it and consider the scheme essential for eradication of the evil of scavenging and for developing a healthy social order.

7. AT THE BOTTOM OF INDIAN SOCIETY : By *Stephen Fuchs*, Munshiram Manoharlal Publishers Pvt. Ltd., New Delhi, 1981

The Nature of Untouchability

The situation of untouchables has changed for the better in recent times. Distance pollution is no more practised, public conveniences are only partly denied to them and many agencies extend economic and moral assistance to them. But the basic disabilities still prevail and the untouchables themselves still suffer from their social degradation. In many places where they try to assert their human rights, they are pitted against the caste Hinds and many atrocities are committed to instil fear in them and to put out any hope in them for an improvement of their lot.

Scavenging Castes

The names of the scavenging castes suggest that they are a functional community recruited from many different ethnic groups. Some of them might have been compelled to take up this occupation by the society to which they belonged, others were reduced by economic necessity to have recourse to it. There are great variations in the physical appearance of the different sections of the respective communities. This may be accounted for by the varied recruitment from higher castes of 'broken men', outcastes, destitutes, etc., and illegitimate connections between scavengers and their employers.

About half of the Bhangis are Hindu, the other half Muslim. But often they mix both religions, reciting prayers from the Koran while also worshipping the Hindu deities. They have a caste council which settles their disputes and imposes fines for misconduct. Most of the Bhangis earn their livelihood by staying in their traditional occupation though some from the younger generation have tried to break away from their caste occupation and learn other trades. In the big cities and industrial centres they have a better chance to succeed in this effort.

8. STRIVING FOR ECONOMIC EQUALITY: By *B.V. Pandya*, Popular Prakashan, Bombay, 1959

Scavenging and sweeping is done exclusively by a particular caste, *viz.*, the Bhangi who are at the bottom of the social ladder. Even among the Harijans, there are 'high' and 'low' but the Bhangi is the lowest of all. Every caste has the privilege of regarding other castes as inferior to it, but not so the Bhangi or his counterpart, the Halalkhor of upper India, the Dom of Bihar and the Madaru of Madras.

The Bhangi caste is indigenous to Gujarat so much so that they are found in small numbers in every village of Gujarat. In the district of Ahmedabad, the municipalities and Gram Panchayats of various talukas had a large majority of the local *Bhangis* with few exceptions here and there.

The system of recruitment in the municipalities differed to some extent and excluding the Ahmedabad City Corporation no other municipality or Gram Panchayat maintained a waiting list of the scavengers and sweepers.

The scavengers and sweepers employed by the Municipality are provided with other benefits in the form of payments in kind. There is slight variance in respect of these in the different talukas of the district. Viramgam and Dholka Municipalities give one half-pant, one shirt and one cap to the male conservancy staff, while the females get one saree and one blouse per year. Dehgam Municipality gives only one piece of bar soap to each worker every week, but no clothes. Ahmedabad City Corporation is somewhat liberal and gives each male worker a pair of half-pants, a pair of shirts and two caps per year. In addition to this, those who remove refuge are given a pair of shoes. The female staff gets two sarees, two blouses and two petticoats every year. The Corporation does not give soap or towel to its conservancy staff.

In earlier days the Bhangis were the only persons engaged in the occupation of scavenging and sweeping. Recently, a number of persons from other communities have entered this field. Thus, we find Hindus, Muslims, Pathans and Christians employed for driving refuge lorries, while Bhangi are employed for driving nightsoil trucks in the city of Ahmedabad. The Bhangi being on the last rung of the social ladder are, however, not allowed to enter a number of occupations by the higher castes, while other persons are entering their limited sphere of activity.

With the advancement of educational facilities, members of the Bhangi community will be in a position to make themselves eligible for certain hitherto inaccessible posts, but it is desirable that the general public should give them sympathetic treatment and have generous outlook towards this class of downtrodden masses who are on the last rung of the social ladder.

9. SOCIAL AND ECONOMIC CONDITION OF URBAN SANITARY WORKERS: A CASE STUDY OF MANGLORE CITY: By *Mohammed Peer*, National Seminar on Action Sociology and Liberation of Scavengers, New Delhi, 1992

An attempt has been made to evaluate the socio-economic status of the scavengers and the impact of different welfare programmes. The obstacles in their progress, measures for ameliorating the conditions of scavengers and tackling the problem of sanitation in general have also been discussed.

Methodology

The universe for the study is Manglore City. With the help of questionnaire a sample of 50 Paura Karmikas (scavengers) was interviewed. This was supplemented by observation and group discussion.

Findings

1. A significant majority of the Paura Karmikas in all the talukas of Dakshina Kannada are Koraga who are a Scheduled Tribe.
2. The Koraga in general are still living in illiteracy, ignorance

and poverty. The condition of the sanitary workers is better.

3. An awareness about the importance of education has been emerging among them. Although substantial proportion of the sample respondents are illiterate, they are sending their children to schools. Free education, scholarship, special incentives given to them by the municipalities have contributed to the growth of awareness about the importance of education among them.
4. Even though the respondents expressed satisfaction with their present occupation, they preferred occupations other than 'sanitary worker' for their children.
5. They have access to temples and also move closely with the members of other communities.
6. The sanitary workers usually suffer from malaria, typhiod, T.B. and skin diseases. There are a few instances of elephantiasis. However, more than half of them said that they have no health problem.
7. Mortality among them is high compared to the general mortality rate. Majority of them die in the age group of 45-55 mainly because of T.B. The mortality rate is higher among males than females.
8. All of them, including women and children, are addicted to drinks.
9. The N.G.Os have not played any significant role in bringing about transformation among this group.
10. The practice of carrying nightsoil on the head is officially abolished, the flush-out system of latrines has also enabled them to improve their status.
11. Their condition is slowly improving in the area under study.

10. OCCUPATIONAL MOBILITY AMONG BHANGIS OF BHOPAL: By *S.N. Choudhary* and *Ravindra Singh*, National Seminar on Action Sociology and Liberation of Scavengers, New Delhi, 1992

The study seeks to find out the trends of inter- and intra-generational occupational mobility and its consequences for the

Bhangis with following objectives :

1. To find out the trends of inter- and intra-generational occupational mobility.
2. To identify the causes and processes of occupational mobility.
3. To analyse the consequences of mobility on psychology, status, attitudes and values.
4. To know the views of mobile Bhangis for acceleration of occupational mobility.

Methodology

The universe for the study is the city of Bhopal. With the help of semi-structured interview schedule sixty male heads of such households were interviewed as have already entered non-caste occupations. Group discussion was also organised.

Findings

From demographic and attributional point of view the Bhangi of Bhopal are not a monolith. The number of illiterates are however higher among the older population than among the younger. Majority of them have left caste occupation but a significant number of them are in between the caste occupation and white-collar jobs. This is primarily because of lack of higher vocational education.

The male functional leaders of the households who are relatively young and educated have all shifted from the caste occupation. They left it because of availability of other jobs and the social and cultural stigma attached to the traditional work.

It is apparent that marriages in recent past have not broken the linkage between caste occupation and illiterate boys and girls of the Bhangis.

In order to assert their superior status among the caste members, neighbourhood, office and friend circle the mobile Bhangi have also changed their traditional dresses, living style, language and surnames.

Promotion of education, generation of social awareness, provision of more and more employment opportunities can definitely promote inter- or intra-generational occupational mobility among the Bhangi.

11. AN OVERVIEW OF SCAVENGERS' PROBLEM : By *Archana Sinha*, National Seminar on Action Sociology and Liberation of Scavengers, New Delhi, 1992

The scenario of scavengers in rural and urban areas is different. The scavenging class living in towns work under municipalities, corporations, hospitals, colleges, hostels, nursing homes and such other institutions. They, therefore, are englightened enough to form their own organisations and trade unions. In case of an increase of confrontation with their employers, they show their mettle without any hesitation. In rural context, the principle of 'co-operate ranking' prevails over individual ranking and the status is collectively defined. Similarly, the working conditions and the method of work of the scavengers are totally different.

12. LIBERATED MUSLIM SCAVENGERS OF BIHARSHARIF: By *S. Musi Raza*, National Seminar on Action Sociology and Liberation of Scavengers, New Delhi, 1992

The Muslim scavengers are also called *Bhangis*. The other names for this group among Muslims are Lalbegi, Mehtar, Sheikh Mehtar and Halalkhor.

After liberation, the situation has changed. The curse of untouchability is being gradually removed. Some social interactions have started with poor Muslim families of lower strata. In certain cases, they are invited by lowly placed Muslims on certain occasions and they also invite them. But such interactions are not free and on a large scale. The Ashrafs and the well-placed Atrafs do not regard them as untouchables, but avoid social intercourse.

The economic condition of this section of Muslim community continues to be miserable. Some of the male members of their families are striving in different directions for earning a livelihood. They are working as *Khalasi*, Tempo and Car driver and semi-skilled mechanics. This is a good trend, but still not strong and much effective in improving their economy. It appears that in case the government pays attention to this deprived section and extends them the facilities given to their Hindu counterparts, their social, cultural and economic conditions may considerably improve and along with liberation from the sub-human occupation, they may attain liberation in socio-cultural and economic spheres.

13. REHABILITATION OF SCAVENGERS IN BIHAR: AN EVALUATION OF POLICIES AND PROGRAMMES:

By *Ravindra Kumar Verma* and *Ramesh Chandra Choudhary*, National Seminar on Action Sociology and Liberation of Scavengers, New Delhi, 1992

For the liberation of scavengers plan allocations were made for conversion of dry latrines into water seal latrines but the allocations were too paltry to mitigate the problem in the beginning. Side by side the Special Component Plans were also earmarked for their rehabilitation but the allocations for SCPs have been reduced from 37 per cent in Seventh Plan to 25 per cent in Eighth Plan.

In view of the present living and social conditions of liberated scavengers the situation leads us to suggest that it is high time to make them socially conscious. Their political awareness has also to be improved in order to make them aware of their rights so that they may grab their claims from the system. They (scavenging communities) should be properly informed about the welfare schemes launched by the government. Besides, the policies and programmes launched by the government ignore two vital aspects, first the rural scavengers and second the women scavengers. The government will have to chalk out programmes for the liberation and rehabilitation of rural and women scavengers.

14. SCAVENGERS AND THE REHABILITATION PROGRAMMES: A STUDY OF IMPACT IN THE MUZAFFARPUR DISTRICT OF BIHAR: By *Jagdish Prasad* and *Anirudh Prasad*, National Seminar on Action Sociology and Liberation of Scavengers, New Delhi, 1992

It is encouraging to note that the rehabilitation programmes have resulted in creating a positive impact on generating employment and increasing earnings of the liberated scavengers. This may be due to wide coverage of the scavenger beneficiaries under various self-employment schemes with the help of the subsidy and credit made available to them. Thus, rehabilitation programmes for the scavengers need to be all-pervasive covering all sections of the Harijan community. The need is to provide initiative and incentives to the scavengers for seeking training and self-employment with assistance from government and non-government agencies. Since this involves motivational change and dynamism on the part of the scavengers, non-government agencies can play a very important role in this respect because of their predilection for involvement in the welfare of disadvantaged masses.

3

RESEARCH OPERATIONS

The inhuman and degrading practice of scavenging is a stigma on our entire social system. This occupation is not only degrading and hazardous but also poorly remunerated. The traditional attitude of the scavengers and the rigid caste structure of the Indian society deprives them of liberty and equality enshrined in the Constitution for all sections of society. In recent years, many efforts have been made by the Government and NGOs for their uplift, yet the actualization of human rights in our own society has been inevitably a slow process. The aim of the present study is to diagnose the existing socio-economic condition of the scavengers in relation to socio-economic variables through an empirical enquiry.

Objectives of the Study

1. To study the working conditions of scavengers still engaged in this profession and to analyse their social disabilities.
2. To analyse the impact of various welfare programmes geared to their liberation and total development during pre- and post-independence periods through the efforts of Government and NGOs.
3. To ascertain the success and failures of rehabilitation strategies adopted for scavengers liberated from this profession.
4. To bring out the implications of the changing scenario from the point of view of human rights.
5. To focus on sociological significance of bringing scavengers from the margin to the mainstream of the Indian society by

abolishing discriminatory attitudes, values and humanitarian ethos of human times.

6. To highlight the gender differences in scavenging since cleaning toilet is a women's job and to study the impact of *Bhangi Mukti* on their psyche.
7. To suggest ways and means to empower the scavenging community with a view to satisfy their political aspirations. At present they are not able to do so on account of smallness in their numbers.
8. To find out why the recommendations of the committees and commissions appointed earlier to go into the problem have not been acted upon.

Methodology

A descriptive research design has been devised and with the help of this a complete picture of the socio-economic condition of the scavengers has been drawn. Thus, the present study aims to describe accurately the characteristics of a group in tune with the objectives drawn.

Universe of the Study

Bihar is the universe for the study. In rural and urban set-up the norms and values attached with scavenging are different. They have a bearing on the employer/employee relationship and working conditions. Both these areas have been covered.

Sampling Design

As mentioned in the first chapter, the total number of scavengers in Bihar as estimated by the Planning Commission's report of 1989 is 22,400, out of which 90 per cent are in urban areas and 10 per cent in rural areas. For the study, 10 per cent sample has been taken from the urban area which comes to 2,016 and 20 per cent from the rural area which comes to 448. To make it in round figure, 2,000 samples from the urban area and 450 samples from the rural areas have been drawn. Therefore, for the present study the sample size is 2,450.

Urban samples are divided into four categories, *viz.*, (a) cities with more than one lakh population, (b) towns with less than one lakh but more than 50 thousand population, (c) towns with population less than 50,000 but more than 20,000, and (d) towns with population less than 20,000. Out of the total 2,000 urban samples, 5 per cent samples are drawn from category A, 30 per cent from category B and 10 per cent from category C and D respectively. This demarcation in the selection has been done keeping in view the high density of the scavengers' population in the big cities.

In the rural areas, 250 samples have been covered from north Bihar villages and 200 from central Bihar villages. Rural areas of tribal Bihar have been left out as scavenging is almost negligible there.

Purposive sampling has been used to select the samples in different categories, picking the right cases in appropriate places which can be used to meet the research need. Further, an effort has been made to cover almost half of the sample size from the female category.

Table 3.1 : Distribution of Rural and Urban Samples in Relation to Selected Area According to Different Categories

URBAN SAMPLES

Category A (50% Sample)			Category B (30% Sample)		
1.	Patna	150	1.	Nawadah	100
2.	Ranchi	150	2.	Kishanganj	100
3.	Jamshedpur	100	3.	Khagaria	100
4.	Dhanbad	100	4.	Bettiah	100
5.	Gaya	100	5.	Gopalganj	100
6.	Bhagalpur	100	6.	Deoghar	100
7.	Muzaffarpur	100			
8.	Darbhanga	100			
9.	Purnea	100			
		1,000			600

Table 3.1 *(Contd.)*

Category C (10% Sample)		Category D (10% Sample)	
1. Lakhisarai	40	1. Marhora (Saran)	40
2. Baulia (Rohtas)	40	2. Jhajha (Jamui)	40
3. Jhanjharpur	40	3. Jagdishpur (Bhojpur)	40
4. Dumraon (Buxar)	40	4. Rajgir (Nalanda)	40
5. Sheikhpura	40	5. Raxaul (E. Champaran)	40
	200		200

RURAL SAMPLES

North Bihar (250 Samples)		Central Bihar (200 Samples)	
1. Bagha (West Champaran)	50	1. Tilothu (Rohtas)	40
2. Sarisabpahi (Madhubani)	50	2. Arwal (Jehanabad)	40
3. Shahpur Patori (Samastipur)	50	3. Kharagpur (Munger)	40
4. Nirjamapur (Begusarai)	50	4. Koath (Buxar)	40
5. Murliganj (Madhepura)	50	5. Dhanarua (Patna)	40
	250		200

Primary Data

The primary data regarding the study has been collected through interview schedule, interview guides, observation notes, group discussion and case studies.

Interview Schedule

There is one schedule constructed for the interview of the respondents. The contents of the interview schedule are in keeping with the objectives of the study. The interview schedule sought to find out information in regard to issues like households, working conditions, impact of welfare programmes, gender issues in scavenging, political empowerment, rural scavenging scenario and suggestions for improving the situation.

Interview Guide

Interview guides were used for persons and agencies who were directly associated with the scavenger community. The Head of Municipal Corporation/Nigam, Head of SC/ST Financial Corporation, District Welfare Officer, office-bearers of NGOs and opinion leaders among scavengers were interviewed to seek information regarding working conditions, implementation of welfare programmes, availability of tools for scavenging, their own personal view regarding change if any in the scavenger community and their suggestions for the same.

Observation

Observation method has been used in the present study to supplement the data collected through schedules and interview guides. The observation points in the present study mainly consist of information regarding position of scavengers' residential locality, their life-style and source of entertainment, their own sense of cleanliness after returning from work, their behaviour after heavy drinking, impact of Government and non-Government welfare programmes, supply of mechanical tools by Municipal Corporation/Nigam and sanitation and environment, condition of the localities where they reside. An effort has been made to observe these variables in real life setting.

Group Discussions

Throughout the field work several group discussions with opinion leaders and others were arranged. In every area covered under the study an effort was made to discuss with the opinion leaders of the scavenger community. These opinion leaders were queried about different issues involved in the study. The information gathered from them has been used in different chapters of the present report.

The purpose of conducting a group discussion was to include the community view regarding different aspects of every-day life in the present study. These group discussions were open for all and participation of female participants was encouraged. The investigator's role was to act as a facilitator, stimulating the participants with new points. An effort was also made to involve a number of people in the group discussion and not allow one or two persons to monopolise the interview. The group discussion was aimed to gather information on the following issues :

1. Opinion of people belonging to other community about scavengers.
2. Opinion of scavengers about people of other community.
3. Nature and type of work performed.
4. Practice of child labour in their community.
5. Efforts made by NGOs for their upliftment.
6. Attitude of Government officials towards scavengers.
7. Awareness about state and national political development.
8. Awareness about drug addiction, AIDS and population control.
9. Availability of potable drinking water.
10. Nature and type of drinking water.
11. Attitudes towards female education.
12. Reaction of their community on the abolition of head loading and change in the design of toilets.

Case Studies

Nine case studies have been made to provide flesh and blood to our research. These case studies were made to unravel some intimate aspects of their life and their perception of changes taking place in their social milieu.

The themes for case studies are as follows :

1. Community Case Studies

(a) Rajasthani scavengers of Ranchi.

(b) Muslim scavengers of Biharsharif.

2. Perception of Change

(a) Old and experienced leaders.
(b) Rural women elite.
(c) Educated urban elite.
(d) Resurgent youth.

3. Problem-oriented Case Studies

(a) Indebtedness.
(b) Drunkenness.

Secondary Data

Secondary data has been collected from available literature such as official reports and other published and unpublished materials in this field. Published materials related with the present study in the context of Bihar are conspicuous by their absence.

Field Experience

Researchers went to the field for data collection in rural and urban areas for survey of socio-economic condition of the scavengers. One investigator was assigned to each area. After reaching the field, he visited the Municipal Corporation/Nigam Office and district headquarters of Sulabh International. These were the two agencies from which information about concentration of scavengers was obtained. Once the area was located, the investigator used to contact the opinion leaders of the community, who, in most cases, worked as resource persons for the field. Rapport with the respondents was established with the help of these resource persons. Investigators explained the objectives of the study to the respondents. The respondents did not understand the purpose of this research. The investigators explained clearly that they belonged to the Sulabh

Institute of Development Studies, Patna, but the respondents presumed that they were from the Government. They thought that their names and the family details noted by the investigators will be submitted to the Government. Respondents were more interested in the feasibility of the welfare programme and were least concerned with the objectives of the study. During group discussion it was noticed that some people always tried to dominate the discussion. On many occasions, women's participation in group discussion was poor.

Government officials were sometimes not available when contacted and in most of the cases the information available from Municipal Corporation/Nigam Office was not up-to-date.

Respondents' Expectations

Respondents' expectations were very high. Scavengers working in Municipal Corporation/Nigam demanded their salary on time rather than mechanical tools. Some complained about the officials' hostile behaviour and expected the investigators to sort out their problems. Respondents who were serving in private houses complained about low payment and hazardous working conditions. Women were eager to know whether they will get the red card. Scavengers working in the Government and private sector both were equally enthusiastic to obtain loan to be provided to them under different scheme apart from good housing facility and proper education for their children.

4

PROFILE OF RESPONDENTS

The profile of the respondents is an important aspect of any field study. It reveals the nature and characteristics of the sample, the age, religion, marital status, type of family, total number of family members and income of the respondents and their migration etc. Through this the socio-economic status of respondents emerges. The rural-urban differential and overall situation is revealed through the tables.

Table 4.1: Age of Respondents

(N = 2450)

Age Group Years	Urban			Rural			Total		
	Male	Female	Total	Male	Female	Total	Male	Female	Total
Below 18	0.4%	0.2%	0.3%	—	—	—	0.3%	0.2%	0.2%
19-35	29.4%	36.8%	32.7%	36.3%	40.3%	38.0%	30.8%	37.5%	33.8%
36-50	49.8%	44.7%	47.6%	52.2%	51.1%	51.5%	50.0%	46.0%	48.2%
51 and above	20.4%	18.3%	19.4%	11.5%	8.6%	10.5%	18.9%	16.3%	17.8%
Total	100%	100%	100%	100%	100%	100%	100%	100%	100%

Table 4.1 reveals agewise distribution of respondents in rural and urban areas of Bihar. Majority of the male and female respondents belong to 36-50 age group. Hardly 0.2 per cent are below 18 years of age. So far as 51 and above age group is concerned the overall percentage is 17.8 per cent. But percentage is just half in the rural areas of this age group of 51 and above. Maximum number of respondents belonged to the age group of 19-35 and 36-50.

Table 4.2: Marital Status of Respondents

(N = 2450)

Marital Status	Urban			Rural			Total		
	Male	Female	Total	Male	Female	Total	Male	Female	Total
Married	93.11%	87.41%	90.06%	94.02%	93.75%	94.00%	93.31%	88.63%	91.22%
Unmarried	1.25%	0.23%	0.08%	0.83%	0.00%	0.44%	1.18%	0.18%	0.74%
Widow	0.00%	12.36%	5.45%	0.00%	6.25%	3.12%	0.00%	11.01%	4.90%
Widower	5.64%	0.00%	3.15%	4.97%	0.00%	2.44%	5.51%	0.00%	3.14%
Total	100%	100%	100%	100%	100%	100%	100%	100%	100%

Notes : 1. Column percentage compares sex based marital status.

2. Total of each row is 100.

Table 4.2 highlights the marital status of the respondents in the rural and urban areas. Most of the respondents in both the urban and rural areas were married. Overall 0.74% of the male and female sample were unmarried. Among the respondents, 4.9% females were widows while 3.1% males were widowers. 0.8% respondents were unmarried in both urban and rural areas. No female respondent in rural area was unmarried.

Table 4.3: Religionwise Break-up of Respondents

(N = 2450)

Religion	Urban			Rural			Total		
	Male	Female	Total	Male	Female	Total	Male	Female	Total
Hindu	98.12%	98.86%	98.45%	100%	99.52%	99.78%	98.47%	98.99%	98.69%
Muslim	1.88%	1.14%	1.55%	0.00%	0.48%	0.22%	1.53%	1.01%	1.31%
Total	100%	100%	100%	100%	100%	100%	100%	100%	100%

Notes : 1. No Sikh and Christian.

2. Column percentage compares religion on the basis of area and sex on grand total.

3. Total of each row is 100.

Table 4.3 reveals the religionwise distribution of respondents in the urban and rural areas of Bihar. There was no Sikh and Christian scavenger in the surveyed area. Although Muslim scavengers were found but their percentage was very low. In the rural area except 0.5 per cent who were Muslim, the rest were Hindu. Overall 98.69 per cent respondents were Hindu while 1.31 per cent were Muslim.

Table 4.4 : Castewise Distribution of Respondents

(N = 2450)

Caste	Urban			Rural			Total		
	Male	Female	Total	Male	Female	Total	Male	Female	Total
Mehtar	43.9%	45.0%	44.3%	31.2%	24.8%	28.2%	41.0%	41.0%	41.0%
Dom	43.3%	43.6%	43.4%	68.7%	75.0%	71.7%	47.0%	49.0%	48.0%
Uraon	0.4%	0.3%	0.4%	00.0%	00.0%	00.0%	0.3%	0.2%	0.3%
Halalkhor	1.6%	1.3%	1.5%	00.0%	00.0%	00.0%	1.3%	1.1%	1.2%
Munda	0.8%	0.5%	0.7%	00.0%	00.0%	00.0%	0.6%	0.4%	0.5%
Dusadh	0.3%	0.2%	0.7%	00.0%	00.0%	00.0%	0.2%	1.0%	0.6%
Chamar	0.7%	1.1%	0.9%	00.0%	00.0%	00.0%	0.5%	0.9%	0.7%
Bansfor	2.6%	1.2%	2.0%	00.0%	00.0%	00.0%	2.2%	1.0%	1.6%
Bin	2.7%	2.8%	2.8%	00.0%	00.0%	00.0%	2.2%	2.2%	2.2%
Bansi	0.08%	0.2%	0.1%	00.0%	00.0%	00.0%	0.07%	0.1%	0.1%
Suri	0.4%	0.4%	0.4%	00.0%	00.0%	00.0%	0.3%	0.3%	0.3%
Hari	1.3%	0.5%	1.0%	00.0%	00.0%	00.0%	1.8%	1.1%	1.5%
Dhapra	1.4%	1.3%	1.4%	00.0%	00.0%	00.0%	1.1%	1.1%	1.1%
Total	100%	100%	100%	100%	100%	100%	100%	100%	100%

Table 4.4 highlights the castes of respondents. The major castes among the scavengers in Bihar are Dom, Mehtar, Halalkhor, Lalbegi, Bansfor, Dhapra, Hari, Rout, Balmiki, Mallick, Kannojia and others. Marwari scavengers are found in some towns of Bihar. Halalkhor are Muslim scavengers working in some places. In Biharsharif women Halalkhor are working as scavengers. Overall majority of the scavengers are Mehtar and Dom. These two castes comprise 89 per cent of the scavengers in the surveyed area. The percentage of Uraon, Halalkhor, Munda, Dusadh, Chamar, Bansfor, Bansi, Suri, Hari and Dhapra is very low. Dhapra caste was found only in Deoghar district

of Bihar.

Table 4.5(A): Type of Family

(N = 2450)

Types of Family	Urban					Rural	All
	A	B	C	D	All		
Nuclear	66.1%	76.0%	77.5%	77.5%	71.35%	81.5%	73.3%
Joint	33.9%	24.0%	22.5%	22.5%	28.65%	18.5%	26.7%
Total	100%	100%	100%	100%	100%	100%	100%

Table 4.5(B): Rural-Urban Distribution

(N = 2450)

Types of Family	Urban	Rural	All
Nuclear	71.35%	81.50%	73.30%
Joint	28.65%	18.50%	26.70%
Total	100%	100%	100%

Table 4.5 brings out the fact that 73 per cent respondents belonged to nuclear family while only 27 per cent were living in joint family. In the rural area 81.5 per cent scavengers were living in nuclear family while 18.5 per cent in joint family. In the urban area 71.35 per cent belonged to nuclear family while 28.65 per cent to joint family. This shows the lower percentage of joint family in both the rural and urban areas.

Table 4.6(A): Family Size of the Respondents

(N = 2450)

Total Number of Family Member	Urban					Rural	All
	A	B	C	D	All		
Below 5	17.4%	24.6%	34.0%	21.5%	21.9%	34.9%	24.2%
6-8	44.1%	51.6%	44.0%	53.0%	47.2%	50.7%	47.9%
8+	38.0%	23.6%	22.0%	25.5%	30.9%	14.5%	27.9%
Total	100%	100%	100%	100%	100%	100%	100%

Table 4.6(A) highlights the family size of the respondents in urban and rural areas. Altogether 24 per cent respondents were having a family size of below 5 members. It means 76 per cent respondents were having large family size. 47.9 per cent respondents were having a family of 6-8 members and 27.9 per cent were having more than 8 members in the family. In the rural area approximately 35 per cent respondents were having a family size of below 5 and 51 per cent of 6-8 and 15 per cent having more than 8 family members.

Table 4.6(B): Family Size of the Respondents

(N = 2450)

Types No. of Family Members	Urban	Rural	All
Below 5	21.90%	34.90%	24.20%
6-8	47.20%	50.70%	47.90%
8+	30.90%	14.50%	27.90%
Total	100%	100%	100%

This shows the prevalence of large size family among the scavengers. About 31 per cent of the respondents from the big cities/ towns were also having more than 8 members in the family. Hardly 22 per cent respondents reported family size of below 5 in the urban area and 78 per cent were in the category of more than 5.

Table 4.7(A): Incomewise Distribution of Respondents

(N = 2450)

Income Category per Month	Urban					Rural	All
	A	B	C	D	All		
Upto Rs. 2000	21.6%	19.8%	46.0%	23.0%	23.6%	66.7%	31.5%
Rs. 2001-4000	50.0%	66.0%	48.5%	69.5%	56.6%	33.3%	52.3%
Rs. 4001-6000	27.0%	14.0%	5.5%	7.0%	19.0%	0.0%	15.5%
Rs. 6000 +	1.3%	0.0%	0.0%	0.5%	0.7%	0.0%	0.5%
Total	100%	100%	100%	100%	100%	100%	100%

Table 4.7(B): Incomewise Distribution of Respondents (Urban-Rural Differential)

(N = 2450)

Income per Month	Urban	Rural	All
Upto Rs. 2000	23.65%	66.70%	31.50%
Rs. 2001-4000	56.65%	33.30%	52.30%
Rs. 4001-6000	19.00%	0.00%	15.50%
Above Rs. 6000	0.70%	0.00%	0.50%
Total	100%	100%	100%

Table 4.7 shows the incomewise distribution of the respondents. 66 per cent respondents are in below Rs. 2000 income group in the rural area which reflects higher concentration of poverty in the rural areas. No household in the income level of more than Rs. 4000 was found in the scavengers of rural area. On the contrary above Rs. 4000 income level was found in the urban area. Although it is hardly 16 per cent but when it is compared with the rural area, it is noteworthy that all respondents belong to urban area. Altogether 31.5 per cent respondents belong to income level of upto Rs. 2000 and only 23.65 per cent from the urban categories. Similarly 52.3 per cent were in the income group of Rs. 2001 to 4000 in which 56.6 per cent were from urban categories and only 33.3 per cent were from rural area. Only 19 per cent respondents belonged to income bracket of Rs. 4001 to 6000 and all of them reside in urban area. Similarly income level of more than Rs. 6000 is reported by only 0.5 per cent respondents all of which were from the urban sector. In the urban categories 93 per cent respondents in the bracket of above Rs. 6000 belonged to A category which is large town. Nobody reported income level of above Rs. 6000 in the small towns (B and C categories). This table indicates that higher income group of people are only in the larger towns and lower income group in the rural areas. The majority of the scavengers are in the urban areas. They have migrated from rural areas in search of employment. Halalkhor of Biharsharif and Marwari scavengers (Balmiki) from Rajasthan came from their native villages many generations back.

In this chapter the caste, age, religion, marital status, type of family, number of members and income have been discussed. Muslims are also engaged in this profession; they are called Halalkhor. The Marwari scavengers, Dom, Mehtar, Lalbegi, Bansfor, Dhapra, Hari are the major castes engaged in this profession. Majority of the scavengers came from nuclear families. Large-sized family is a characteristic of the scavengers in Bihar. Due to lack of education and better health facilities people desire more children When their children are sick they prefer to go for traditional health care than to doctors. Diseases are caused by witches is the belief of both the rural and urban scavengers.

The scavengers are still in the grip of poverty. The income level is low. Only in the big cities some scavengers were in the higher income group but their percentage was only 1.3. Altogether 0.5 per cent scavengers were in the income group of above Rs. 6000. Owing to poverty they do not have basic facilities like water and sanitation.

The details of living and working conditions of scavengers are discussed in the following chapter.

5

LIVING AND WORKING CONDITIONS

Living and working conditions are one of the best indicators of status of any community. In this chapter an attempt has been made to highlight the ownership of the house, basic facilities, nature of work, earning members, supplementary work, pattern of expenditure, indebtedness, saving habit, adoption of family planning, means of entertainment and income. The social disabilities and socio-cultural constraints and relationship with the people belonging to other castes and people in the same profession have also been discussed. All these features have been discussed on the basis of findings given in a number of tables.

Table 5.1: Incomewise Distribution of House Ownership

Income Group	Urban	Rural	All
Own			
Below 2000	48.40%	51.50%	32.50%
2001 to 4000	84.80%	15.00%	51.00%
4001 to 6000	100%	0.00%	16.00%
Above 6000	100%	0.00%	0.40%
	75.50%	24.50%	100%
Total	53.50%	77.00%	58.00%

(Contd.)

Table 5.1 : *(Contd.)*

Income Group	Urban	Rural	All
Rented			
Below 2000	100%	0.00%	11.42%
2001 to 4000	100%	0.00%	71.42%
4001 to 6000	100%	0.00%	17.14%
Above 6000	0.00%	0.00%	0.00%
Total	100%	0.00%	100%
	1.80%	0.00%	1.40%
Government Quarters			
Below 2000	79.60%	20.30%	31.00%
2001 to 4000	92.50%	7.50%	53.50%
4001 to 6000	100%	0.00%	14.80%
Above 6000	100%	0.00%	0.70%
Total	90.00%	10.00%	100%
	44.70%	23.00%	40.70%
Grand Total	81.63%	18.37%	100%
	100%	100%	100%

Table 5.1 highlights the incomewise distribution of households as well as ownership of house among the scavengers. This table indicates that house ownership is high in rural as compared to urban areas. Maximum number of 'own' houses were found in the rural areas while in urban areas all the respondents were living in rented houses. So far as government quarter and government land is concerned 90% of urban scavengers live in government quarter/ government land. Altogether 58% live in houses of their own while 1.4% in rented house and 40.7% in government quarter/government land. In the rural areas 77% live in 'own' house and the rest in government quarters. It was observed that the surroundings of the houses of scavengers were very dirty. Bad odour came out of filth and heap of garbage. In many houses there was only one room where five to six family members have been living.

In many places the Corporation provided one-room accommodation for scavengers. They have to pay Rs. 150 to 165 per

Table 5.2(A): Incomewise Availability of Water Facilities to the Respondents

Category Income	Drinking Water								
	Tap		Handpump		Well		Pond		All
	Personal	Community	Personal	Community	Personal	Community	Personal	Community	
	1	2	3	4	5	6	7	8	9
Urban									
Below 2000	2.14%	22.90%	1.00%	59.00%	0.20%	10.00%	0.00%	2.90%	20.00%
2001 to 4000	2.70%	20.00%	2.00%	61.00%	0.60%	10.90%	0.30%	2.30%	56.00%
4001 to 6000	2.40%	29.00%	1.80%	56.50%	1.50%	6.30%	0.00%	1.50%	23.00%
Above 6000	0.00%	33.00%	4.70%	52.00%	0.00%	9.50%	0.00%	0.00%	0.30%
Total	2.50%	23.00%	1.90%	59.50%	0.70%	9.80%	0.00%	2.30%	100%
Rural									
Below 2000	0.00%	0.00%	1.10%	82.00%	0.20%	16.30%	0.00%	0.00%	66.20%
2001 to 4000	0.00%	0.00%	9.20%	74.20%	0.00%	16.50%	0.00%	0.00%	32.10%
4001 to 6000	0.00%	0.00%	100%	0.00%	0.00%	0.00%	0.00%	0.00%	1.50%
Above 6000	0.00%	0.00%	0.00%	0.00%	0.00%	0.00%	0.00%	0.00%	0.00%
Total	0.00%	0.00%	5.30%	78.30%	0.10%	16.10%	0.00%	0.00%	100%

(Contd.)

Table 5.2 (A) : (*Contd.*)

	1	2	3	4	5	6	7	8	9
All									
Below 2000	1.25%	13.33%	1.62%	68.74%	0.25%	13.06%	0.00%	1.70%	28.40%
2001 to 4000	2.47%	17.88%	2.81%	62.50%	0.62%	11.58%	0.00%	2.10%	51.60%
4001 to 6000	2.40%	28.80%	3.30%	55.70%	1.50%	6.20%	0.00%	1.80%	15.00%
Above 6000	0.00%	33.00%	5.00%	52.00%	0.00%	9.50%	0.00%	0.00%	0.70%
Total	2.00%	18.80%	2.50%	63.00%	0.60%	10.90%	0.30%	1.90%	100%

month as house rent but there was no facility at all. Corporation does not care about these quarters. The situation is so bad that accident can take place any day. There was one such case in Pathal Kudua Mohalla in Ranchi town. Although Rs. 25,000 was shown in the repair head by the Corporation no repair work was visible.

Most of the Municipal Corporations and Municipalities do not maintain the quarters of scavengers.

Table 5.2(A) deals with the availability of basic facilities like drinking water in relation to income of the respondents. Overall 20% people use tap, 65% handpump, 11% well and hardly 2% take water from pond for drinking purposes in the urban areas. Only 2% scavengers use personal and 18% community taps while 2.5% use personal and 63% community handpumps for drinking purposes. The percentage of users of wells is scarcely 10% for drinking purposes in the urban areas. There was no tap in the houses of scavengers in the rural areas. In the rural areas majority of the scavengers use handpumps for drinking purposes in comparison to other sources of water like wells and ponds. Neither personal nor community tap was available for drinking purposes in the rural areas.

It was found that in some towns scavengers have no facilities for drinking water. Even in cities like Jamshedpur, there was scarcity of drinking water. Although there are handpumps, most of them were defunct. In some places scavengers had to fetch water from distant places. Bath is also a problem for them. Sometimes they do not take bath due to shortage of water.

In Nawada some scavengers fetched water from the tap located at the Railway platform. They have no bath and drinking water facilities in their hamlet.

Scavengers of Mundichak Bhatta (a hamlet in Bhagalpur town) fetch water from a distance of half kilometre. They do not have drinking water facilities nearby. The same situation exists in Doranda Manitola in Ranchi. They have to fetch water from government tap of Tipudana road which is located half a kilometre away. There is a government tap 100 metres away. But that tap has been monopolised by others. A government well was constructed in the Harijan colony of Doranda Manitola but Municipal Corporation staff has fenced the godown in whose compound the well is located. Scavengers of this

Table 5.2(B): Incomewise Distribution of Drainage Facilities

(*N* = 2450)

Category Income	Urban			Rural			All		
	Kachcha	Pucca	Total	Kachcha	Pucca	Total	Kachcha	Pucca	Total
Below 2000	76.00%	24.00%	61.20%	99.10%	1.00%	38.70%	85.00%	15.00%	35.66%
2001 to 4000	72.00%	28.00%	88.30%	98.60%	1.40%	11.69%	75.00%	25.00%	52.36%
4001 to 6000	52.60%	47.30%	100%	0.00%	0.00%	0.00%	52.70%	47.30%	15.50%
Above 6000	61.50%	38.50%	100%	0.00%	0.00%	0.00%	61.50%	38.50%	0.50%
Total	70.00%	30.00%	81.60%	99.00%	1.10%	18.30%	75.00%	25.00%	100%

colony use the well only from 7 a.m. to 12 p.m. as the godown remains closed after that time.

Table 5.2(B) reveals the distribution of drainage facilities of the respondents incomewise. 99% drainage was kachcha in rural areas while it was only 70% in urban areas. Altogether 75% drainage was kachcha while 25% was pucca. Incomewise distribution indicates that as income increases the percentage of pucca drainage increases. As income increases, the incidence of kachcha drainage diminishes. But the availability of pucca drainage in the rural areas is meagre as 99% drainage was kachcha. The state of drainage is very bad in most of the cities in Bihar. Municipal Corporations do not pay attention to drainage. The situation is so bad that the High Court has passed strictures for cleaning of drainage for the solution of waterlogging in Patna town.

The condition of drainage is bad in every town. It was observed that drains were being used by the children for defecation. There was waterlogging due to lack of drainage in the Jarlahi Mohalla of Bhagalpur. Similarly, the situation of drainage was bad in other towns also. Filth and garbage were scattered near houses. That is why the surroundings were very dirty. At some places stagnant water was found due to lack of drains. Drains have not been constructed under Minimum Needs Programme of the Government.

Table 5.2(C) brings out the availability of personal and community toilets in scavengers households. In the urban category scavengers have more personal toilets while there was no personal toilet in the rural area. The percentage of personal toilet is very low even in the urban areas (8.75%). Higher the income the higher is the number of toilets in the house. Some members of higher income group also use community toilets as well as open space for defecation. Altogether 73% scavengers use open space for defecation. In the urban areas it was found that 63.7% scavengers do so. Approximately 28% scavengers use community toilets. It was found that there were no community toilet facilities in the smaller towns (C and D categories) and the entire rural area in Bihar. In the rural areas, open field, orchard and riverside are used as places for defecation. In the urban areas people use road, railway track, river and open field for this.

Table 5.2(C): Toilets Facility Available

(N = 2450)

Income Group	Personal	Community	Open Space	Total
Urban				
Below 2000	3.80%	9.70%	84.30%	23.65%
2001 to 4000	8.00%	26.70%	66.20%	56.15%
4001 to 6000	16.80%	52.60%	30.50%	19.00%
Above 6000	28.50%	35.70%	35.70%	0.70%
Total	8.75%	27.60%	63.70%	100%
Rural				
Below 2000	0.00%	0.00%	100%	66.66%
2001 to 4000	0.00%	0.00%	100%	33.33%
4001 to 6000	0.00%	0.00%	0.00%	0.00%
Above 6000	0.00%	0.00%	0.00%	0.00%
Total	0.00%	0.00%	100%	100%
All				
Below 2000	2.30%	6.00%	91.50%	100%
2001 to 4000	6.90%	23.30%	69.60%	100%
4001 to 6000	16.80%	52.60%	30.50%	100%
Above 6000	28.00%	35.70%	35.70%	100%
Total	7.10%	22.50%	73.20%	100%

Either there is no arrangement of toilets or the condition of toilets was bad in most of the towns. Consequently, children use drains and roadside for defecation. This was the situation of scavengers' hamlets in Ranchi, Jamshedpur, Bhagalpur, Jhajha, Purnea and even Patna.

Scavengers of Harmoo colony in Ranchi reported that one community toilet of 10 seats had been constructed by Sulabh International. But the Municipal Corporation has made no arrangement for its maintenance.

Table 5.2(D): Availability of Electricity

(N = 2450)

Category Income	Urban			Rural			All		
	Yes	No	Total	Yes	No	Total	Yes	No	Total
Below 2000	27.40%	72.50%	100%	29.00%	71.00%	100%	28.00%	72.00%	100%
2001 to 4000	51.00%	49.00%	100%	25.00%	75.00%	100%	48.00%	52.00%	100%
4001 to 6000	74.00%	26.00%	100%	0.00%	0.00%	0.00%	74.00%	26.00%	100%
Above 6000	77.00%	23.00%	100%	0.00%	0.00%	0.00%	77.00%	23.00%	100%
All	50.00%	50.00%	100%	28.00%	72.00%	100%	46.00%	54.00%	100%

Table 5.3: Medical Facilities Available

(N = 2450)

Category Income	Urban			Rural			All		
	Male	Female	Total	Male	Female	Total	Male	Female	Total
PHC / Hospital	21.20%	22.00%	21.55%	18.18%	14.42%	16.45%	20.66%	20.55%	20.61%
Private Practice	70.57%	68.27%	69.55%	66.76%	64.42%	66.22%	70.07%	67.59%	68.94%
Both	2.06%	3.74%	2.80%	0.42%	0.48%	0.44%	1.77%	3.11%	2.37%
No Response	6.17%	6.00%	6.10%	13.64%	20.58%	16.88%	7.50%	8.81%	8.08%
Total	100%	100%	100%	100%	100%	100%	100%	100%	100%

As many as 50% of the sample households among the scavengers in urban, 28% in rural areas and altogether 46% have electricity. So far as incomewise distribution of electricity-holders is concerned, in the urban area 74% of Rs. 4001-6000 income group and 77% of above Rs. 6000 income group have electricity in their houses while 27.4% of income level below Rs. 2000 have electricity. This shows that higher the income level the higher is the percentage of electric connections in the house.

Altogether 54% scavengers of urban and rural areas do not have electricity. Thus, most of the scavengers still lack this facility.

Table 5.3 highlights the medical facilities available to the scavengers sexwise in the urban and rural areas. Scarcely 20.61% respondents availed the medical facilities through the Government hospital or PHC. Majority of the respondents reported private facilities like nursing home, clinic, quack and registered medical practitioners. 2.37% respondents reported both the private and public hospital/PHC etc. 8% of the sample size gave no response.

This table indicates that approximately 69% people availed of private medical facilities in both the urban and rural areas. In the urban areas about 21% availed of medical facilities from either Government hospital or PHC. 69.55% respondents availed private source of medical facilities. Only 2.80% respondents reported both the facilities while 6.10% gave no response. In the rural areas only 16.45% scavenger respondents reported that they availed of medical facilities from Government hospital or PHC. 66.22% respondents of the rural areas reported having availed the facilities of the private clinic and private practitioners.

The percentage of no response by the females was maximum in the rural areas. 44.42% of the rural female respondents used the Government hospital or PHC facilities while 22% urban female respondents did so.

This table shows that scavengers of both the urban and rural areas were served more by private nursing home or private clinic rather than Government hospital or PHC.

Table 5.4: Distribution of Earning Members Incomewise

(N = 2450)

Category	Up to 3 Members Monthly Income			Four and above Members Monthly Income			Grand Total
	Below 4000	Above 4000	Total	Below 4000	Above 4000	Total	
Urban	95.60%	4.40%	6.8%	79.10%	20.90%	93.2%	81.63%
Rural	100%	0.00%	11.2%	100%	0.00%	88.8%	18.36%
Total	96.70%	3.20%	7.6%	82.80%	17.20%	92.3%	100%

Table 5.4 deals with the number of earning members and monthly income in different categories. Approximately 92.3% households have four or more earning members. In the urban areas majority of the respondents are in below Rs. 4000 income group. This shows that there are four and more earning members in the scavengers' family and they have monthly income below Rs. 4000. There are more than four earning members in the rural areas in the income category of below Rs. 2000. No respondents belongs to above Rs. 4000 income group. Although there are four and above earning members in the rural areas but income level has not gone up. This shows urban-rural disparity in income. In the big cities some respondents belong to income level of above Rs. 6000 but in small towns such respondents do not exist.

Scarcely 7% people were found in three earning members category in both the income levels *i.e.* below Rs. 4000 and above. On the contrary the category of four and more earning members accounted for 93% in urban areas. Out of these only 20% belonged to above Rs. 4000 category with earning members four and above. In both the rural and urban categories 82.8% belonged to four and more earning members category in the income level below Rs. 4000. Only 17% respondents were in Rs.4000 and above category with earning members four and above. Out of 7.6% respondents who belonged to three earning members category, 3.2% respondents belonged to the income group of above Rs. 4000.

The monthly income level of above Rs. 4000 is nil in the rural

Table 5.5: Supplementary Occupation of Respondents by Sex

(*N* = 2450)

Category	Male			Female			Total		
	Yes	No	Total	Yes	No	Total	Yes	No	Total
Urban	44.40%	55.60%	55.90%	77.00%	83.50%	41.10%	79.30%	83.40%	81.63%
Rural	48.30%	51.70%	53.77%	23.00%	16.50%	46.22%	20.60%	16.60%	18.36%
Total	45.00%	55.00%	55.51%	39.00%	60.90%	44.18%	42.40%	57.60%	100%

areas while it is lowest in the urban areas as reported by the respondents. It is hardly 21% in those families where earning members were four and above while it is only 4.4.% in those families where earning members were upto 3.

Table 5.5 reveals the supplementary occupation of the scavengers in urban and rural areas. The percentage of supplementary occupation is higher in urban areas *i.e.*, 79.3% while it is only 20.6% in rural areas. Altogether 42.5% respondents reported supplementary occupation in both the rural and urban areas. More supplementary work is available in urban arcas. That is why 80% males and 77% females have taken up supplementary occupation in urban areas while only 20.60% males and 23% females do so in rural areas. Altogether 45% males and 39% females are engaged in supplementary work like basket making, toy making, rag picking and carrying of bricks and other manual work. Scavengers are compelled to do this supplementary work for their livelihood. Majority of the municipal authorities and Notified Area Committees do not regularly pay salary to their staff. Sometimes it is in arrears for months together. This is the main reason which makes them to go for supplementary occupation.

Table 5.6 shows sexwise distribution of income from supplementary work. Altogether 96% scavengers from urban areas earn Rs. 500 per month from supplementary occupation. Only 4% scavenger respondents of urban areas reported income of above Rs. 500 from supplementary work. The condition is the same in rural areas. Overall 96% respondents reported income of Rs. 500 per month from supplementary occupation.

There is male-female difference in the income level in the urban areas. In the rural areas male income above Rs. 500 per month is double that of the females. Hardly 2.5% respondents were in the income level of above Rs. 500 among rural females while it was 5% among rural males. In brief, majority of the people reported that the income from supplementary occupation is upto Rs. 500 per month. Only 4% respondents reported an income of above Rs. 500 per month. The same situation exists with both males and females.

Table 5.7 deals with indebtedness of the respondents in relation

Table 5.6: Sexwise Income of Respondents from Supplementary Occupations

(N = 2450)

Category Income	Urban			Rural			All		
	M	F	Total	M	F	Total	M	F	Total
Up to	56.00%	44.00%	100%	60.00%	40.00%	100%	56.60%	43.40%	100%
500	96.00%	96.00%	96.00%	95.00%	97.50%	96.00%	96.00%	96.00%	95.86%
Above 500	57.00%	43.00%	100%	75.00%	25.00%	100%	58.80%	41.20%	100%
	4.00%	4.00%	4.00%	5.00%	2.50%	4.00%	4.00%	4.00%	4.14%
Total	56.40%	43.60%	100%	60.00%	40.00%	100%	56.80%	43.20%	100%
	100%	100%	100%	100%	100%	100%	100%	100%	100%

Note: Upper percentage shows simple rural, urban and sex composition. Lower percentage denotes male, female, rural, urban comparison on the basis of income.

M = Male, F = Female.

Table 5.7: Indebtedness in Different Income Brackets Sexwise

Urban

(N = 2000)

Category Income	Male			Female			Total		
	Yes	No	Total	Yes	No	Total	Yes	No	Total
Below 4000	69.38%	30.60%	100%	68.46%	31.53%	100%	68.99%	31.00%	80%
Above 4000	69.54%	30.45%	100%	74.11%	25.88%	100%	71.82%	28.17%	20.00%
Total	69.00%	31.00%	100%	70.00%	30.00%	100%	69.50%	30.50%	100%

Rural

(N = 450)

Category Income	Male			Female			Total		
	Yes	No	Total	Yes	No	Total	Yes	No	Total
Below 4000	79.00%	21.00%	100%	81.00%	19.00%	100%	80.00%	20.00%	100%
Above 4000	0.00%	0.00%	00%	0.00%	0.00%	00%	0.00%	0.00%	00%
Total	79.00%	21.00%	100%	81.00%	19.00%	100%	80.00%	20.00%	100%

(Contd.)

Table 5.7: *(Contd.)*

All

Category Income	Male			Female			Total		
	Yes	No	Total	Yes	No	Total	Yes	No	Total
Below 4000	71.28%	28.71%	100%	72.00%	18.00%	100%	71.50%	28.50%	84.00%
Above 4000	69.54%	30.45%	100%	74.00%	16.00%	100%	72.00%	28.00%	16.00%
Total	71.00%	29.00%	100%	72.00%	28.00%	100%	71.50%	28.50%	100%

to income brackets and sex. Majority of the scavengers have been victims of indebtedness. This is a common phenomenon in the urban as well as rural areas. Approximately 70% in the urban and 80% of the rural respondents are in debt. Overall 71.5% scavengers are in this state. It is almost same for male and female respondents. But it differs with income below Rs. 4000 and above Rs. 4000. 80% indebtedness was found in the category of below Rs. 4000 and 20% in the above Rs. 4000 in the urban area.

The main reason behind indebtedness is unemployment, poverty and irregular payment of salarly by the municipal authorities. The other reasons are gambling, alcoholism and social obligations like marriage, food and medicine. The scavengers of Biharsharif reported that they have mortgaged their houses to meet medical expenses. The living condition was also very pitiable due to irregular payment to scavengers by the municipalities. They have to take loan for meeting their survival needs. Sometimes they have to mortgage their beddings, boxes, utensils and clothes when they require money.

The interest rate is very high. It is 25% per month or 300% per annum.

Table 5.8: Sexwise Savings of Respondents

(N = 2450)

Category	Male		Female		Total	
	Yes	No	Yes	No	Yes	No
Urban	53.00%	47.00%	54.00%	46.00%	53.00%	47.00%
Rural	38.00%	62.00%	39.00%	61.00%	39.00%	61.00%
Total	50.30%	49.77%	51.00%	49.00%	50.50%	49.50%

Saving is the most important indicator for development orientation of individuals. Saving habit depends upon the income and other factors like security for the future. Table 5.8 reveals that 50% of the respondents reported saving. Saving habit was more in the urban areas in comparison to rural areas. Approximately 53% of the urban scavengers showed saving tendency while 39% rural scavengers revealed this. Due to low level of income in the rural areas, the propensity to save was low. Similarly, the attitude towards saving among the females was more in comparison with male respondents. In the urban areas, the saving level of males was 53% while it was hardly 38% in the rural areas. Altogether 50% males were in the habit of saving. The figure for females was 51%. The reason behind more saving in the urban areas was that scavengers have higher income level in comparison to rural respondents. In rural areas people are poor and unemployed and they have no regular source of income.

Table 5.9: Employment Position of Respondents by Sex

Sex / Nature of Work	Male		Female		All		Total
	P	T	P	T	P	T	
Urban	58.00%	41.50%	58.00%	42.00%	58.00%	42.00%	100%
	83.60%	80.00%	80.50%	81.00%	82.00%	80.70%	81.63%
Rural	52.80%	47.27%	59.00%	41.00%	56.00%	44.00%	100%
	16.30%	20.00%	19.50%	19.00%	18.00%	19.30%	18.36%
All	57.40%	42.60%	58.00%	42.00%	58.50%	42.50%	100%
	100%	100%	100%	100%	100%	100%	100%

Note : P = Permanent, T = Temporary.

Table 5.9 indicates the sex and nature of work in urban and rural areas. Approximately 58% respondents were in permanent job while 42% are engaged in temporary job in the urban areas. Similarly, 56% are in permanent job and 44% in temporary job in the rural areas. Overall 58% of the respondents are in permanent and 42% in temporary job in the rural and urban areas taken together.

As far as rural-urban differential for males is concerned approximately 84% permanent jobs were in the urban areas while it is hardly 16% in the rural areas so far. Regarding female workers 80% were in permanent job in urban areas and about 20% in rural areas. This means that the majority of permanent female workers belonged to urban areas. Temporary male and female workers are almost equal in both the rural and urban areas. Rural-urban difference is same as among permanent male workers.

Table 5.10: Use of Family Planning Methods by Respondents

Use of Family Planning Method	Oral Pills		Loop		Vasectomy		Tubectomy		Nirodh		Total		Total
	Yes	No	Yes	No	Yes	No	Yes	No	Yes	No	Yes	No	
Urban	1.87%	31.50%	0.50%	32.00%	6.70%	26.70%	17.80%	15.50%	6.50%	26.90%	33.00%	67.00%	100%
	100%	86.00%	100%	87.00%	80.00%	89.00%	86.00%	88.60%	94.00%	85.00%	87.4%	0.00%	81.36%
Rural	0.00%	21.30%	0.00%	21.30%	7.00%	14.00%	12.40%	8.00%	1.70%	19.50%	21.00%	78.60%	100%
	0.00%	14.00%	0.00%	13.00%	20.00%	10.70%	14.00%	11.40%	6.00%	14.00%	12.6%	0.00%	18.30%
All	1.50%	29.60%	0.40%	30.60%	6.70%	24.40%	16.80%	14.30%	5.50%	25.50%	31.0%	69.00%	100%
	100%	100%	100%	100%	100%	100%	100%	100%	100%	100%	100%	100%	100%

Majority of the respondents in category A of the urban sample have a permanent job. Their percentage declines in categories B, C, D, and rural areas. Small towns and rural areas have more temporary staff while large cities have more permanent ones. This shows that scavengers living in the smaller towns are temporary.

We find just the opposite scenario between A and C categories. In the A category 73% respondents were in the permanent job while in the C category 73% have temporary job or are in private work. Majority of them are under-employed. They have to look for work every day.

Table 5.10 highlights the use of family planning methods in urban and rural areas by the scavenger respondents. Altogether 31% respondents used any one of family planning methods like oral pills, loop, vasectomy, tubectomy and *Nirodh* in both the urban and rural areas. As far as urban respondents are concerned, 33% reported the use of these methods while in rural areas it is hardly 21%. This shows that majority of the respondents *i.e.* approximately 80% did not use family planning in the rural areas.

Overall 1.5% use oral pills, 0.4% loop, 6.7% vasectomy, 16.8% tubectomy and 5.5% *Nirodh* as family planning methods. As far as oral pills and loop are concerned only urban respondents were the cent per cent users of these methods. Nobody reported the use of oral pills and loop in the rural areas. Similarly, vasectomy, tubectomy and *Nirodh* were used by 6.7%, 16.8% and 5.5% respondents of urban and rural areas taken together. There is lesser use of these methods by the respondents of rural areas. In rural areas only 1.7% respondents reported use of *Nirodh*, 7% resorted to vasectomy and 12.4% to tubectomy. This shows that family planning methods were practised to a lesser extent in the rural areas.

Table 5.11 deals with the means of entertainment in the scavenger households. Overall 60.6% respondents have radio as a means of entertainment. It is very common in urban areas as well as rural areas, although the percentage of respondents having radio in rural areas is 15% in comparison to 84.70% in urban areas. Out of 60.6% enjoying carrom game only 2% respondents belong to rural areas and the urban percentage is 98%. Video game was available to 0.1% and this was found only in the urban area.

Table 5.11: Means of Entertainment

Mode of Entertainment	Radio	Carrom Board	Video Game	T.V.	Any other	No means of Entertainment	Total
Urban	63.00%	2.40%	0.10%	24.45%	0.20%	9.80%	100%
	84.70%	98.00%	100%	99.00%	83.00%	47.50%	81.63%
Rural	50.00%	0.20%	0.00%	0.80%	0.20%	48.00%	100%
	15.00%	2.00%	0.00%	1.00%	17.00%	52.50%	18.36%
All	60.60%	2.00%	0.08%	20.00%	0.20%	16.80%	100%
	100%	100%	100%	100%	100%	100%	100%

Altogether 20% respondents have TV in their houses but it is mostly in the urban areas. The percentage of respondents having TV in the rural areas was only 1% approximately. 10% respondents in urban areas and 48% in rural areas have no means of entertainment in their houses.

Table 5.12: Relationship of Respondents with Other Castes by Sex

Category	Male		Female		Total		Total
	Yes	No	Yes	No	Yes	No	
Urban	41.00%	14.00%	30.60%	13.50%	71.65%	28.35%	100%
	84.00%	77.00%	83.20%	76.00%	83.80%	76.50%	81.63%
Rural	34.00%	19.70%	27.30%	19.00%	61.00%	39.00%	100%
	15.70%	23.00%	16.70%	24.00%	16.80%	23.50%	18.36%
All	39.70%	15.80%	30.00%	14.40%	69.50%	30.50%	100%
	100%	100%	100%	100%	100%	100%	100%

Table 5.12 highlights the sexwise distribution of respondents and their relationship with people outside their caste. Approximately 72% of urban respondents reported close relationship with the people outside their caste. 61% rural respondents reported having close relationship with other castes. Overall 69.5% respondents of both the urban and rural areas reported close relationship while

approximately 30.5% were having no relationship with the people from other castes. Those who reported close relationship with the people of outside castes, the urban respondents were approximately 83.8% and 16% rural respondents. The male-female difference is also visible from the table. 41% males and 30.6% females had close relationship with other caste people in the urban areas while 34% males in rural areas enjoyed such relationship. 30.6% females in urban and 27.3% in rural areas were having close relationship with the people of other castes.

Table 5.13: Type of Relationship with Outside Scavengers

	Urban	Rural	Total
Male			
Cordial	30.60%	0.00%	19.30%
Normal	67.30%	99.50%	78.90%
Hostile	1.90%	0.50%	1.80%
Total	100%	100%	100%
Female			
Cordial	24.50%	0.00%	19.80%
Normal	73.60%	100%	78.60%
Hostile	1.50%	0.00%	1.50%
Total	100%	100%	100%
Total			
Cordial	28.00%	0.00%	23.00%
Normal	70.00%	99.70%	75.50%
Hostile	2.00%	0.30%	1.60%
Total	100%	100%	100%

Table 5.13 indicates sex and type of relationship with the outside scavengers. Overall 28% of urban respondents reported cordial relation while 70% normal and only 2% hostile relationship with outsider scavengers. In the rural areas 99.7% respondents

reported normal relationship with outsider scavengers. Only 0.3% reported hostile relationship. 99.5% rural male respondents reported normal relationship with outside scavengers. Similarly, all rural female scavengers reported normal relationship with other scavengers. Altogether 17.8% cordial, 73% normal and only 1.6% hostile responses were recorded by male scavengers. Female respondents reported 19.6% cordial, 78.6% normal and 1.5% hostile relationship with other scavengers.

Jajmani Relations of the Scavengers

Caste relations in traditional Indian society were governed by *Jajmani* system. *Jajmani* system is the economic expression of caste. Castes are mutually exclusive, yet they enter into service relationships with one another. These service relations are Jajmani relations. The basic principle behind the Jajmani system is that it makes use of hereditary personal relationships to express the division of labour. Each family has specialised task; secondly, it regulates presentations and counter-presentations in a way which accords with custom for the usual tasks, and mostly the repayment is in kind. In the Jajmani system, the upper castes are *Jajmans* and the lower castes are *Kamins*. Superficially, it is the caste ranking that determines whether one is a *Jajman* or *Kamin*.

In rural areas the scavenger families in the status of Kamin have a fixed zone of work which is known as their customary rights. These customary rights among the scavengers are inherited, purchased and gifted. There is a common practice among the scavengers that at the time of need they can sell or mortgage their work area to another scavenger family. Apart from selling the work area it can also be gifted to other scavengers.

The mode of payment to a scavenger is almost similar to other occupational Kamins. The scavengers are paid in kind and cash and may also be given clothes. Apart from their regular payment they are also entitled to get clothes and food on marriage and other festivals. Frequency of payment in the Jajmani system is not fixed. It may be monthly, half-yearly or annual, depending upon the general trend in the village. Payment in advance by the Jajman to Kamin, both in cash and kind, is also in vogue. The Jajmani system has started withering away under the challenge of the modern age which had dawned in India. It has been marked with centralized government, mass migration, urbanization, the emergence of salaried and wage earning groups and the introduction of money economy on a large scale. This system worked well as long as each village was practically insulated, there was no cash, local economy with few labour alternative and the ultimate power was with the Jajmans.

Table 5.14: Table Showing Action Taken in Case of Encroachment

Rural (N = 450)

Response	Percentage
Stop the person	36.67
Retaliate by Encroaching	4.44
Call Jati Panchayat	23.78
Take up alternative job	0.00
Any other	35.11

Table 5.14 shows the action taken in case someone from outside enters the Jajmani area. About 36.67% scavengers stop the person who tries to enter the Jajmani area. About 4.44% scavengers retaliate by encroaching in other persons's work area. Complaints were made to the jati panchayat in such cases.

Among the scavengers according to the Jajmani rules areas are fixed for the scavengers families. No one else is allowed to serve there. Despite this tradition which has also a legal sanction the problem of encroachment is very common among the scavengers. Generally, it has been noticed that in the absence of working male the area under the command of a family is encroached by other scavengers.

Table 5.15 reveals the changes in the traditional Jajmani system in recent years. 80% respondents in North Bihar were aware of the changes in Jajmani system. In Central Bihar 20% respondents both the male and the female noticed such changes. Now, due to gradual disappearance of Jajmani system the scavengers feel liberated and are free to sell their labour to any rural agency.

Table 5.15: Table Showing Action Taken in Case of Encroachment

(N = 450)

Sex	North Bihar (N = 50)	Central Bihar (N = 250)
Male	108 54.00%	20 50.00%
Female	92 46.00%	20 50.00%
Total	200 80.00%	40 20.00%

In Central Bihar, 80% respondents are of the view that no change has taken place in the Jajmani system and it still persists. Among the scavengers of this area the migration patterns and change of occupation are still slow in comparison to North Bihar.

In the traditional Jajmani system the scavengers constitute an important category of service castes in the Hindu community because it is they who are traditionally responsible for doing unclean work. This Jajman-Kamin relationship was weakened due to the migration and urbanization process. This community found a new prospect in the urban setting as far as choice for occupations is concerned. The stigma of being unclean is also less in the urban areas. In addition, the context of rural economy has undergone such changes probably in all Jajmani relationships.

Summing Up

Basic amenities like housing, drinking water, sanitation, electricity and medical facilities are extremely poor in this community. Very few live in government quarters and these quarters are in bad shape. There is scarcity of proper drinking water due to lack of handpump and tap facility in their locality. Sanitation and electricity facilities are available to very few scavenger families and that also in urban periphery. For health care they mostly rely on quacks and paramedicos.

In every scavenger family almost everybody is engaged in some occupation, either in government sector or otherwise. Despite this, their quality of life is poor owing to the fact that they spend more on unproductive items.

They do not get appliances for performing their duties. Service conditions are also not good. Even Minimum Wage Act is not followed. In Patna, casual labour is given only Rs. 21 per day. Some staff are such who have been working for 10 years but they are paid only Rs. 21 per day. Head loading is still prevalent in some of the towns in Bihar. It is seen in Gaya, Bhagalpur and Purnea and other places. Unemployment and under-employment is the basic characteristic of the scavenger community.

Both men and women are engaged in supplementary work. But this opportunity is available more in urban area where their occupational mobility is higher than in rural area.

Indebtedness is a major problem of this community and the main reason behind it is unemployment, poverty and irregular payment of salary by the Municipal authorities.

Most of the jobs for the scavengers are confined to the urban area. Women in the scavenger community who are residing in urban area take full advantage of their skill due to bulk requirement in the Municipal Corporation.

Still most of the scavengers are unaware of different family planning methods and prefer large-size families. This is mainly due to lack of proper information and the age-old prejudice that large-size family has an economic advantage.

The Jajmani system among the scavengers is still in vogue in some rural areas in northern Bihar. Although there had been some substantial changes in the working and payment conditions, the superstructure remains the same. Occupancy right and its sale and purchase exist as in the past.

The next chapter highlights the human rights and political empowerment of the scavengers in Bihar.

6

HUMAN RIGHTS, EMPOWERMENT AND POLITICAL PARTICIPATION

Human rights are certain fundamental rights that are essential for any human being to lead a normal conflict-free life. Whatever be the theory on which human rights are based their ultimate aim is to grant the individual the necessary freedoms to make his life on this earth worth living with reasonably just comfort and happiness in harmony with others in society.

Development as a Human Right

The concept of human rights is rooted in the most ancient values and religions of our heritage and incorporated into the eminent philosophies and political doctrines of the world. The World Conference on Human Rights in Vienna broke new ground in its recognition of the 'right to development' and the meeting of basic economic and social needs as a fundamental human right. Thus, the Third World view of the interrelatedness of political, economic and social rights was finally accepted.

However, while there was acceptance in principle that alleviation of extreme human poverty and deprivation is central to the meaningful exercise of political and civil rights, there was no agreement on providing the financial means for development to meet economic and social rights. In particular, achievement of the right to universal primary education, to adequate nutrition and health, to employment and minimum wages requires substantial resources.

Human development evolves from basic and universal rights as affirmed in the universal declaration of human rights. As we have seen these rights are of two types:

— Those that relate to basic human well-being such as the right to food, shelter, livelihood and economic security of family and person; and
— Those which protect people from misuse and abuse, including the right to freedom of expression and association and the right to redress of grievances through due process.

Traditional approaches to development which equated development with economic development have been revised and a broader and more comprehensive view of development is steadily being formulated.

The declaration of the right to development was endorsed by the United Nations General Assembly in 1986.

> "The individual is, by virtue of the right to development, entitled to participate in, contribute to and enjoy economic, social, cultural and political development in which all human rights and fundamental freedoms can be fully realized."

We have superceded the domain of economics and entered the realm of the cultural, the social and the political. Development can no longer be assessed within the context of micro and macro economic variables but within the broader cultural context of human rights. A country's development can be more accurately assessed by reference to women's human rights. Women's rights are an essential factor in development and that they need to be addressed directly and not to be swept under the rug of human rights.

It is noteworthy that in the 1993 Vienna Conference on Human Rights eight hundred women groups organised a campaign to press the conference to recognise women's human rights as an integral component of all UN human rights activities. Also their meeting triggered lively discussion about future universal and culturally specific strategies in this context.

The special feature of the struggle in modern times for the

preservation of human rights is that it is now a universal movement and the violations at any place cannot be hidden from others for long. For the first time in the international sphere the U.N. Charter has made the issue of human rights binding on member countries which are required to safeguard them. The Charter makes it obligatory on the part of member states to cooperate with the UN in promoting universal respect for, and observance of, human rights and fundamental freedoms for all, without distinctions of race, sex, language and religion. The rights of the human persons are based on mankind's increasing demand for a decent civilised life in which the inherent dignity of each individual would receive respect and protection.

There is a challenge of well-being. The international human rights community has worked to ensure well-being understood as the right to life and security in combating torture and slavery, arbitrary arrests and extra-judicial executions. These challenges will still be with us. But we now must reformulate the challenge of well-being to include poverty and a basic right to food, health, cleanliness and to shelter. In a world of 5,500 million people, 1,500 million live in absolute poverty. That a child dies of starvation is as much a denial of human rights as when an adult is tortured or forced to suffer the indignity of carrying human excreta on the head. Our notion of well-being in the human rights context must include, in the words of the Irish writer James Joyce from Life's Feast: Scavengers are one such outcaste.

Human Rights of the Dalits after Independence

Since the attainment of independence, India has undertaken one of the most profound reorderings of the society ventured by a democratic nation in modern times. Article 17 of the Indian Constitution which was adopted in 1950 abolished untouchability, a practice rooted in the social and religious life of India for more than 2000 years. This major break with tradition was effected through the inspiration of Mahatma Gandhi and the labour of Dr. B.R. Ambedkar. Article 17 not only forbids the practice of untouchability but declares that enforcement of disability arising out of untouchability shall be an offence punishable in accordance with law. Article 35 provides that Parliament shall have the power to make laws prescribing punishment for those acts which are declared to be offences in this context. In fact, the Parliament exercised this power by enacting the Untouchability Offences Act in 1955. This was amended later and came to be known as the Civil Liberty Act. This Act provides punishment for enforcement of disabilities in regard to entrance and worship in a temple, access to shops and restaurants, practice of occupations and training, use of water sources, place of public worship and accommodation, public conveyance, hospitals, educational institutions, construction of residence or premises, holding religious ceremony, use of jewellery and finery. The imposition of disability is a crime punishable upto Rs. 500, imprisonment upto 6 months, cancellation and suspension of licences and of public grants. As a matter of fact, under Article 15(2) of the Constitution it was provided that no citizen on the ground of only religion, race, caste, sex, place of birth or any of them be subject to any disability, liability or restriction. Article 25 which guarantees freedom to profess, practise and propagate religion is specifically made subject to other fundamental rights provisions and is explicitly qualified by the provision that nothing in this Article shall affect the operation of any existing law or prevent the state making law and providing for social welfare for throwing open of Hindu religious institution of a public character to all classes or sections of Hindus.

Article 29(2) forbids the person in charge of educational institution receiving aid out of state fund to deny admission to an applicant on grounds only of religion, race, caste, language or any of them.

Article 23 prohibits Begar or forced labour. Articles 341 and 342 enjoin the President of India to specify by public notification castes which shall for the purpose of the Constitution be deemed as scheduled castes. This was done by presidential notification in October 1950. This list has been revised many times. Article 46 provides for the promotion of educational and economic interest of the weaker sections with special reference to the scheduled castes and the scheduled tribes.

Article 275 provides for special allotment funds by the Union Government for the welfare of the scheduled castes and scheduled tribes. This was in addition to the sums already provided by the State Government.

Articles 330 and 332 provide for the reservation of seats for the SCs in the Parliament and in the State Legislative Assemblies. Article 335 specifies that at the time of making appointments to the reserved posts, care should be taken to maintain desirable level of efficiency in the services.

Article 338 provides for the appointment of Special Officer by the Union Government to oversee the social welfare programmes being carried out by Central and State Government. The Special Officer was later on designated as the Commissioner for Scheduled Cates and Scheduled Tribes. His main duty was to present an annual report to the President which was discussed in the Parliament. It is a pity that about ten years back this post was abolished by the Government of India and this function is now being exercised by the Commission for Scheduled Castes and Scheduled Tribes.

Although untouchability has been abolished by law and its practice made an offence, it is still to be found in many parts of the country particularly in the rural areas. It has been reported that about 80% of all the cases registered were challened by the police but only half of those challened ended in conviction. The enforcement of the law lies with the State. The law enforcement resources on antidisability enforcement are very low. Very few NGOs are interested in such enforcement. Except in very few disputes involving major issues there has been no organisational support to defend such cases. Among the educated in urban areas untouchability is almost a dead issue. There is no interest of the intellectual community in programmes for attacking untouchability, no debate about alternatives, no assessment of prospects. As a perceptive observer put it 'law means the police and police means higher caste people'. In many cases, police are often uninformed about the provisions of law. Even if the conviction is secured, the penalty is so low as to have little deterrent effect. The aim of such laws is not to prosecute the offender but to promote new patterns of behaviour. On this account too, the Untouchability Offence Act (UOA) 1955 revealed a wide gap between the law of books and law operating. The gap between knowledge and practice is specially true of the prohibitions of the UOA where a fairly large percentage of persons, particularly upper and dominant castes, know the rules but have not changed the practice of untouchability. In many villages higher caste people did not consider practices like denial of use of drinking water from wells, entering into temples and smoking and eating with others as untouchability. In their opinion these practices are a way of life. It has to be realised that social disability is an area in which legislation and administration cannot accomplish much. Basically it is a matter of how people think and what their values are.

With the growing clout of the scheduled castes on account of adult suffrage the government is becoming more responsive to their demands. We may expect the opposition to the Government policies of special treatment for ex-untouchables to become more overt, more articulate and more powerful in coming years.

On account of reservations in services and fast spread of education, it is expected that in villages the incidence of untouchability will drastically go down.

Human Rights of the Dalits

The Scheduled Castes and the Scheduled Tribes (Prevention of Atrocities) Act was passed in September 1989, making illegal some 24 social and economic abuses of the scheduled groups. The Act makes it a criminal offence for legal and administrative proceedings to be deliberately abused by police or security forces in cases involving members of scheduled groups. It allows states to establish special courts to try such cases and provides for legal aid and for compensation for victims of abuse. Dalits and *adivasis* are frequently tortured for political reasons, to deter them or punish them for involvement in organised resistance to economic exploitation. Often adivasi and dalit villages have been raided, and their inhabitants tortured and raped by police acting in collusion with local ruling groups such as landowners. Such abuses are common in Bihar, where most torture victims are landless labourers and their families compaigning for land reform and minimum wages. Landlords have often resorted to violence to suppress such campaigns with the assistance of criminal gangs or private armies. In a number of cases local police officers are alleged to have connived with such groups or even participated in attacks on landless people.

The Special Case of Scavengers

Scavenging is a human rights question because it violates Article 1 (All humans are born free and equal in human dignity and human rights), Article 4 (None will be held in slavery or servitude), Article 5 (No one shall be subjected to cruel, inhuman or degrading treatment or punishment) and Article 23 which says: "Everyone, without discrimination, has the right to equal pay and equal work". Scavenging also violates the preamble of the universal declaration of Human Rights (signed on December 10, 1948) which among other things says: "The Charter affirms faith in the dignity and worth of human person and in the equal rights of men and women. Scavengers, who are made untouchables in their own country, need protection under the Charter not less than the victims of apartheid in South Africa, ethnic conflicts in the Balkans, of the victims of prejudices anywhere else in the world. Scavengers, however, do not get media attention because they have been suffering the indignity of physically cleaning and carrying human excreta for centuries without protest and with total resignation".

One of the features of the Indian caste system is that each caste has been associated with a particular occupation. The so-called superior castes enjoy a wide range of choices which the lower castes do not. The lowest castes do unclean jobs, the two main tasks are sweeping and leather processing. Sweeping streets, cleaning drains and sewers, removal of human and animal waste, raising pigs etc., are their jobs. Since latrines in most cities do not have flush, the sweepers or scavengers (Balmikis) have to carry buckets of human faeces on the head. Leather work includes handling of dead animals, removing their skin and curing it, and making leather goods. By assigning these tasks to these people, soeicty has saved other people from doing dirty work. The jobs that Dalits do are not only undesirable, polluting and hard, but are also low paid.

Legislation on Abolition of Scavenging

Parliament passed the Employment of Manual Scavengers and Construction of Dry-latrines (Prohibition) Bill, 1993 to abolish scavenging and ban the construction of dry latrines. This was, no doubt, a historic decision but no time limit had been given, by which the system of manual scavenging would be totally abolished and thus, the very purpose of the Bill was defeated. The states of Andhra Pradesh, Goa, Karnataka, Maharashtra, Tripura and West Bengal have adopted this Act by passing a resolution in their respective Assemblies. The Government of India constituted a seven-member (including Chairperson and Vice-Chairperson) National Commission for Safai Karamcharis under the National Commission for Safai Karamcharis Act, 1993 in August 1994. The tenure of the Commission is three years. The main function of the Commission is to recommend to the Central Government specific programmes of action towards elimination of inequalities in status, facilities and opportunities for *Safai Karamcharis* under a time-bound action plan, study and evaluate the implementation of the programmes and schemes relating to social and economic rehabilitation of Safai Karamcharis.

People's Commission on Abolition of Scavenging

In spite of many Commissions and Committees including the National Commission for Safai Karamcharis set up in 1994, the degrading practice of manual scavenging still continues. Hence Sulabh has set up People's Commission on abolishing scavenging which will take a holistic view of the problem and suggest ways to abolish it. The terms of reference of the proposed Commission are to ascertain the nature and extent of the problem of manual scavenging in its historical and contemporary perspectives; to determine the extent to which manual scavenging has been reduced in the country, to develop a socio-economic profile of scavengers in rural and urban areas; to examine the working and living conditions of scavengers; to find out the participation of scavengers in education and other development programmes; to study and evaluate the effectiveness of various schemes on the abolition of manual scavenging; and to make recommendations for the scavengers with a view to finally abolish this practice totally.

Present Scenario of Discrimination, Oppression and Awareness among Scavengers in Bihar

The position of the scavengers has not improved much. The majority of the scavengers are engaged in the lowest type of unskilled work like sweeping. They have been treated as untouchables. It is an old proposition that the profession of *Bhangis* is lowest in caste hierarchy. Blunt has drawn attention to such a factor operating in the past, "eleven castes will not touch a Bhangi". He further adds that "being touched by such an untouchable required a good Hindu to bathe himself and wash his clothes". Dumount's study also indicates that out of a total of 25 untouchable castes there are twelve which do not touch the Bhangi. Hutton places the Bhangi castes in the lowest grade of Hindu social system.

In Bihar, majority of the scavengers are living in towns and cities, although there is improvement in the social status of scavengers due to conversion of dry latrines into pour flush by the Sulabh International. In the cities and bigger towns their working conditions have improved but in some places the manual removal of nightsoil is still persisting. Head-loading is still in practice in some of the towns of Bihar. The prevalence of discrimination, oppression and awareness among scavengers in Bihar has been explored in the following tables dealing with the experience of untouchability, ban on entering temples, awareness of liberation scheme for the scavengers by the Government and corporate efforts by the scavengers themselves for their betterment.

Table 6.1: Distribution of Sexwise Experience of Untouchability

Category	Sex				Total		
	Male		Female				
	Yes	No	Yes	No	Yes	No	Total
Urban	34.65%	21.25%	26.50%	17.60%	61.15%	38.85%	100%
Rural	34.40%	19.33%	27.55%	18.66%	62.00%	38.00%	100%
All	34.61%	20.89%	26.69%	17.79%	61.30%	38.69%	100%

Table 6.1 highlights the experience of untouchability by the respondents in urban and rural areas. 61.30% respondents felt that untouchability exists in society. They have experience of untouchability in day-to-day life. Both male and female respondents have experience of untouchability. This shows that untouchability is still prevalent in society in both rural and urban areas. Males in rural and urban areas have experienced it more than females. Overall 34.61% males and 26.69% females had experience of untouchability.

The table shows that majority of the respondents had suffered discrimination frequently. Those members of the community who have achieved success in some fields or might have link with politics of administration are not discriminated against in society. Sulabh International played a vital role in the upliftment of the scavengers by promoting attitudinal changes in society.

The attitude of the youths towards scavengers has changed now. The youth in the urban areas sit together and take tea with them. But older people still hesitate to do so. Scavengers feel that there is decline in the incidence of untouchability. Among the scavengers, sweepers do not want to marry their children with those of head-loaders (manual scavengers).

Not only higher castes even scheduled caste people discriminate against scavengers in the society. Similarly, Rikshaw-puller scavengers do not have contact with the head-loader scavengers and the Chamar, Dusadh, Pasi, Dhobi and other scheduled castes also discriminate against the scavengers.

Table 6.2: Ban on Temple Entry

Category	Sex				Total		
	Male		Female				
	Yes	No	Yes	No	Yes	No	Total
Urban	20.55%	35.45%	13.65%	30.45%	34.20%	65.80%	100%
Rural	8.00%	45.77%	4.22%	9.33%	12.22%	87.77%	100%
All	18.20%	37.26%	11.51%	32.57%	30.16%	69.83%	100%

Table 6.2 indicates the incidence of ban on temple entry. In the urban areas prohibition was more than double in rural areas. In the urban areas males were more affected than females. Only 8% males and 4.22% females had this experience in the rural areas.

Scavengers are being deprived of the right of temple entry. This is a gross violation of human rights in the society. There is discrimination in the society towards scavenging community.

Table 6.3: Awareness about Liberation of Scavengers

Category	Sex				Total		
	Male		Female				
	Yes	No	Yes	No	Yes	No	Total
Urban	25.65%	30.25%	16.35%	27.75%	42.00%	58.00%	100%
Rural	11.33%	42.44%	5.33%	40.88%	16.66%	83.33%	100%
All	23.02%	32.48%	14.32%	30.16%	37.34%	62.65%	100%

Table 6.3 brings out the extent of awareness about liberation of scavengers by the government. Majority of the respondents were unaware of the 'Liberation of Scavengers' scheme by the government. Only 37.34% were aware of the liberation scheme. Awareness was higher in the urban areas. Urban females were more aware than rural females. Urban males were also more aware than rural males. Altogether 23.02% males and 14.32% females were aware of the scavengers liberation programme. Awareness in the

rural areas was about 16.66%.

This shows poor awareness regarding liberation programme for the scavengers in the rural areas. Although the scheme of 'Liberation of Scavengers' was started by the Ministry of Home Affairs in 1980-81 under PCR Act with the twin objectives of conversion of existing dry latrines into pourflush latrines on the whole town approach basis in the selected small and medium towns, and rehabilitation of liberated scavengers in alternative dignified occupations, it suffered a great setback after it was transferred to the Ministry of Urban Development and HUDCO with the modified financial pattern. The Ministry of Social Justice and Empowerment has launched Training and Rehabilitation Programme for the liberation of scavengers.

But respondents have almost no knowledge regarding the Liberation of Scavengers Programme of the Government.

Table 6.4: Corporate Efforts for the Liberation of Scavengers

Category	Sex				Total		
	Male		Female				
	Yes	No	Yes	No	Yes	No	Total
Urban	2.14%	58.90%	0.70%	38.27%	2.85%	97.14%	100%
Rural	0.00%	68.00%	0.00%	32.00%	0.00%	100.00%	100%
All	1.96%	59.67%	0.65%	37.70%	2.62%	97.37%	100%

Table 6.4 highlights the collective efforts for the liberation of scavengers. Hardly 2.6% respondents knew about any corporate efforts for liberation. No attempt has been made in the rural areas. Only urban respondents among the scavengers knew about it.

Scavengers have no forum, no union, no caste leader to plead for their salvation. They are defenceless people almost perpetually waiting for a redeemer who does not seem to be coming. In spite of many commissions and committees including the National Commission for Safai Karamcharis the degrading practice of manual scavenging still continues.

Sulabh has set up the People's Commission on abolition of

scavenging which will take a holistic view of the problem and suggest ways to abolish it. Sulabh International, Ambedkar Institute of Research and Rehabilitation, Yarpur, Patna, Sulabh Institute of Research and Rehabilitation, Khajpura, Patna are the important NGOs doing a lot of work for the uplift of the scavengers.

Table 6.5: Persons Approached in Case of Physical Assault

(N = 2450)

Person Approached	Urban			Rural			Total
	Male	Female	Total	Male	Female	Total	
Influential Persons	50.89%	49.32%	50.20%	73.97%	75.96%	74.89%	54.73%
Go to Police Station	42.75%	43.31%	43.00%	19.42%	15.86%	17.78%	38.36%
Higher Officer	2.16%	1.93%	2.05%	0.00%	0.00%	0.00%	1.60%
Any Others	4.20%	5.44%	4.75%	6.61%	8.18%	7.33%	5.22%
Total	100%	100%	100%	100%	100%	100%	100%

Table 6.5 points out the persons approached in case of physical assault on the scavengers. Dalits are a vulnerable section of the society. Atrocities on Dalits are common in Bihar. It is more in rural than in urban areas. In urban areas also they are being oppressed by the society. The vulnerability of Dalits led to many deaths in custody as a result of torture and brutality. Deaths of Dalits in police custody are particularly common in certain states.

In the urban area half of the sample respondents approached influential people while approximately three-fourth of the sample respondents did so in rural areas. Altogether more than half of the sample size of both the urban and rural areas contact influential persons at the time of physical assault. Less than half of the respondents of the urban areas go to the police station. But in the rural areas less than one-fourth of the respondents report to the police station in case of physical assault. Nobody contacts higher official in the rural areas.

This shows that majority of the respondents do not report to police station in case of physical assault.

Table 6.6: Police Response to the Scavengers' Complaints

Area	Sex				Total		
	Male		Female				
	Yes	No	Yes	No	Yes	No	Total
Urban	25.70%	30.20%	19.70%	24.40%	45.40%	54.60%	100%
Rural	16.22%	37.55%	12.44%	33.77%	28.66%	71.33%	100%
All	23.95%	31.55%	18.36%	26.12%	42.32%	57.67%	100%

Table 6.6 deals with steps taken by the police on complaints. About one-third of the respondents were satisfied that police was responsive to their complaints. It was higher in the urban areas. Overall 42.32% respondents were satisfied with the police step whenever complaint was lodged.

Majority of the respondents of rural areas reported that no steps were taken by the police on scavengers' complaints. The same was also the case in the urban areas.

Political Empowerment of Scavengers

In 1979 India ratified the International Covenant on Civil and Political Rights that came into force in 1976. This covenant and the Covenant on Economic, Social and Cultural Rights which constitute a detailed codification on human rights have legal force as treaties between the parties thereto.

Article 7 of the International Covenant on Civil and Political Rights prohibits acts of torture and of cruel, inhuman or degrading treatment or punishment. Article 10, provides that "All persons deprived of their liberty shall be treated with humanity and with respect for the inherent dignity of the human persons". Article 5 of the UN Declaration of Human Rights, 1948, also lays down that "No one shall be subjected to torture or to cruel, inhuman or degrading treatment or punishment".

Political means are another way whereby the lower castes have striven to raise their economic and social status. The dilemma for the lower castes has been whether to work along with the upper castes or separate from them, under the banner of scheduled castes parties.

British rule and Western education awakened Indians to the need for social reform and political freedom. Social reformation preceded organised political consciousness, the two went together for a time but precedence was given to political struggle against the alien rule. Despite the rule of law, under the British the lower castes continued to suffer from social disabilities in varying degrees. Gandhi had done much for the untouchables. Controversy arose between Ambedkar and Gandhi regarding safeguards for the depressed classes. Gandhi was opposed to separate electorate for the depressed classes.

The scheduled castes are conscious of their importance in the democratic process. They are approached for support by the various political parties. Contrary to the election laws the political parties exploit the religious sentiments, caste and linguistic susceptibilities of the voters. This is all the more so in the case of the reserved seats. It is observed that caste sentiments do play a part in the selection of candidates and in voting behaviour.

Some *Bhangis* have made successful political careers mainly through reserved seats in local municipal bodies and metropolitan council. They depend largely on upper and middle caste voters. They, however, can confidently rely on their own caste voters who act as a block. Once they win they are merged into the world of privileges, amenities and influence which is a complete departure from their previous low social status. They are frequently re-elected in the elections. They are incorporated into the political establishment. Such Bhangi elite suffer a dual isolation. They are no longer at the level of their community. They tend to distance themselves from their broader ethnic base. At the same time they are not accepted fully by the upper caste fellow politicians. The main body of caste remains in the slum.

Older Bhangi leaders are less ambitious than the younger ones. The latter are more politicised, better educated and more aware.

Casteism is denounced by most political parties and yet they covertly appeal to caste factors in electioneering. It is held that scheduled caste candidates elected on party ticket speak for their parties, rather than for their downtrodden people. Some of the scheduled caste leaders become willing tools of the political parties dominated by the upper castes. There is no reason to believe that politics in the reserved constituencies is any different from what it is in the general constituencies.

There is a widespread belief among the Bhangi that they are not getting a fair share in the political process. According to them, their community has only a small representation and influence in local affairs. Bhangis consider themselves as the chosen ones of Mahatma Gandhi. In the world of real politics party tickets at election time go to those most likely to win election. Bhangis are a minority group among the various scheduled castes. The Chamar, Dusadh, Pasi and Dhobi are more powerful. Mehtar and Dom are marginalised in Bihar. They do not figure in scheduled caste politics.

Representation of Scheduled Castes in Legislature

The Constitution has provided for reservation of some seats in Parliament and State Assembly constituencies for scheduled castes and scheduled tribes in proportion to their population in each state. The reservation is made under Articles 230, 332 and 334 of the Constitution. This reservation was initially for a perod of 10 years and subsequently extended by 10 years at a time by amending Article 334 of the Constitution in 1959, 1969 and then again in 1980. Perhaps the framers of the Constitution thought that the period of 10 years would be enough for bringing the under-privileged groups at par with the rest of the society. The aim of these protective measures is to make the under-privileged groups self-reliant with the passage of time.

According to the provision of the Delimitation of Parliamentary and Assembly Constituencies Order 1976 scheduled castes were allotted 8 seats in Lok Sabha and 46 seats in Legislative Assembly in Bihar.

Contrary to the election laws, the political parties exploit the religious sentiments, caste and linguistic susceptibilities of the voters. This is all the more so in the case of the reserved seats. It is a general observation that caste sentiments do play a part in the selection of

Table 6.7: Sexwise Political Affiliation

Affiliation of Respondents	Urban			Rural			Total		
	Male	Female	Total	Male	Female	Total	Male	Female	Total
As a Voter	98.92%	97.39%	98.25%	99.58%	100%	99.77%	99.03%	97.88%	98.53%
Not Interested	1.07%	2.60%	1.75%	0.41%	0%	0.22%	0.07%	2.12%	1.46%
Total	100%	100%	100%	100%	100%	100%	100%	100%	100%

candidates and in voting behaviour. While it is true in the case of reserved constituencies the practice is fairly common even when other minority religious groupings are concentrated in constituencies. In the case of reserved constituencies, it is a general practice that other things being equal the candidate should be from the scheduled castes in the partcular constituency. Candidates are selected on the basis of their vote-getting ability in their constituencies.

Table 6.7 reveals the political affiliation of the respondents. In urban male category majority of the respondents participated in political activity as a voter and 1.07% showed no interest. Nobody participated as candidate in the rural and urban areas. Very few urban females showed any interest in political activity. Overall 1.46% respondents showed no interest in political activity. Most of the respondents participated as voters in the rural areas. Majority of the voters belonged to the income level of below Rs. 4000 in the urban areas. Nobody was found with income level of above Rs. 4000 in the rural areas.

This shows lack of leadership aspiration among the scavengers. Other than voting in an election, they keep themselves away from other political activities like working for a party as party worker etc. Females are more shy in Bihar and their participation is less than desired. Illiteracy, non-awareness, poverty are the main reasons.

Politically Dalits tend to be of marginal importance. Dalits remain, by and large, neglected. In fact, "It is only the upper and middle caste groups, with resources of wealth and numbers, that have enjoyed the fruits of caste-oriented democracy while the lower castes have been for all practical purposes outside the political arena" (Harry W. Blair, 1979).

Table 6.8 brings out the fact that among all the respondents mostly favoured BJP followed by RJD and Congress. Only rural respondents with income below Rs. 4000 prefer BJP, RJD followed by BSP and Congress respectively.

BJP is more popular among the respondents who are in the income group of below Rs. 2000 per month. One of the interesting findings of the study is that the influence of BSP and Communists who champion the cause of Dalits is almost negligible whereas the BJP is emerging as a powerful force against Congress and RJD in a traditional Congress citadel. RJD is popular among higher income group members in urban areas.

Table 6.8: Incomewise Distribution of Respondents by their Political Performance for Political Parties

Party	Income						All
	Urban			Rural			
	4000	4001+	Total	4000	4001+	Total	
Congress	14.00%	5.07%	12.30%	7.77%	0.00%	7.77%	11.46%
BJP	64.70%	44.09%	60.85%	51.11%	0.00%	51.11%	59.06%
Samata	0.87%	2.53%	1.20%	4.00%	0.00%	4.00%	1.71%
RJD	15.19%	40.86%	20.25%	24.66%	0.00%	24.66%	21.06%
BSP	0.06%	0.00%	0.05%	8.44%	0.00%	8.44%	1.59%
C.P.I.	1.05%	2.28%	1.30%	1.11%	0.00%	1.11%	1.26%
Janata Dal	1.93%	3.55%	2.25%	2.88%	0.00%	2.88%	2.36%
Regional Parties	2.05%	0.76%	1.80%	0.00%	0.00%	0.00%	1.40%
Total	100%	100%	100%	100%	100%	100%	100%

Summing Up

Human dignity, human rights and fundamental freedom, equality, equity and social justice constitute the basic values in all societies. The pursuit, promotion and protection of these values among others provides the basic legitimacy of all institutions and promotes an environment in which human beings are centre of concern for sustainable development. They are essential to a healthy and productive life in harmony with nature. The question of human dignity and human rights is specially important in the context of women. "Without progress in the situation of women, there can be no true social development. Human rights are not worthy of the name if they exclude the female half of humanity. The struggle for women's equality is part of the struggle for a better world for female human being, and all socieities" observed Mr. Boutros Ghali, former Secretary General of the United Nations.

In Bihar the Sulabh Sanitation Movement began in 1972. It

seeks to create a new social dispensation where men and women may live together as partners in progress. Dr. Bindeshwar Pathak has worked relentlessly to abolish scavenging, restore human rights to scavengers, 70% of whom are women and create a new sanitation order. However, head-loading is still in existence in many towns of Bihar such as Gaya, Bhagalpur and Purnea. Children below the age of 14 years have changed their profession and are now engaged in picking of paper plastic, polythene. Virtually they have been deprived of education and health facilities. Parents are not at all interested in educating their children.

In India, women scavengers who have been carrying on the practice of manual scavenging, generation after generation, face humiliation, only to be treated and scorned as untouchable due to the abject poverty in which they live and the caste structure which has confined them in a vicious circle. Even today as we approach the twenty-first century, seven lakh scavengers, 70% of whom are women, have yet to be freed from this task.

Now some scavengers are enjoying human rights with human dignity. The first effective step in this direction was taken by the Sulabh Shauchalaya Sansthan (now Sulabh International Social Service Organisation). There has been some impact of liberation on the social prestige enjoyed by the liberated scavengers, in respect of visit to temples, engagement of Brahmins to supervise religious ceremonies, invitation by other caste people on ceremonial occasions taking water from common places along with other caste people and taking food in hotels and other places. It proves that liberation has enhanced their social prestige and hence they are allowed to visit those temples in which upper castes go for worship. But still scavengers are looked down upon not only by higher castes but by scheduled caste people also.

Political empowerment is the need of the society but in practice due to lack of education, awareness and resources scavengers have not been empowered politically. They are small in numbers and in a democracy where voting numbers count they do not have much of a chance. These two factors marginalised the scavenger community in the process of political empowerment. Although they have equal political rights, they do not participate in the political process as other scheduled castes like Dusadh, Pasi, Chamar and Dhobi do. Scavengers are at the bottom of the community. They are lowest amongst scheduled castes. Many families do not find their names in voters lists.

Although they have been benefited by the Training and Rehabilitation Programme of the Ministry of Social Justice and Empowerment, the rehabilitation process is very slow. Bihar State Scheduled Castes Development Corporation has not spent grants given by the Government of India under the GARIMA Programme for the scavengers.

Sulabh persuaded the Ministry of Home Affairs, Government of India, to include the liberation of scavengers and their rehabilitation programme on the whole town approach basis under the scheme "Implementation of PRC Act" in 1980-81 and two towns of Bihar *viz.*, Biharsharif and Purnea, were taken up for the first time in India. In 1982-83 three more towns of Bihar, namely, Daltonganj, Chaibasa and Madhubani, were taken up. Later, the programme spread to other states. The Ministry of Welfare, Government of India, later took charge of this programme.

They participate in the democratic process as voters. Very few contest the elections. The reason for this is lack of caste-based voting strength. In addition to this, they cannot afford the finance necessary for fighting elections. They can contest Panchayat and Municipal Ward elections. They are not much interested in political activities.

The Government of India constituted National Commission for Safai Karamcharis in 1994 for evaluating and implementing the programme and scheme relating to the social and economic rehabilitation of *Safai Karamcharis*. This Commission has the potentiality to speed up the upliftment programmes for the scavenger community.

Sulabh International Social Service Organisation has set up the People's Commission on abolition of scavenging which will take a holistic view of the problem and suggest ways to abolish it. This will help provide human dignity, human rights, political participation and empowerment of Dalits, particularly the scavenging community.

7

RECOMMENTATIONS OF COMMISSIONS AND COMMITTEES

Article 15 of the Constitution of India prohibits discrimination on grounds of religion, race, sex or place of birth. The Directive Principles of State Policy in Article 46 provide that the State shall take steps for promotion of educational and economic interests of scheduled castes and other weaker sections of the people such as scavengers and sweepers etc.

In order to make constitutional provisions effective, a number of Committees and Commissions had been constituted by both the Central and State Governments, from time to time, for the welfare of the scavenger community. Some of the main committees and commissions constituted by the Central and State Governments are as follows :

1. *Barve Committee* (B.C.) : The esrtwhile Government of Bombay appointed a committee known as the Scavengers' Living Conditions Enquiry Committee in 1949 with Shri V.N. Barve as Chairman to inquire into the condition of scavengers in the State of Bombay. The committee submitted its report to the Government of Bombay in 1952.
2. *Backward Classes Commission* (B.C.C.) : The Backward Classes Commission was appointed by the Government of India in 1953 under the chairmanship of Kaka Kalelkar which submitted its report in 1955. The observations and recommendations of the commission were brought to the notice of the State Governments by the Ministry of Home Affairs in

October 1956.

3. *Malkani Committee* (M.C.) : The Central Advisory Board for Harijan Welfare a body under the Ministry of Home Affairs, Government of India, constituted a committee, known as Scavenging Conditions Inquiry Committee, under the chairmanship of Prof. N.R. Malkani in 1957. The committee started its work in January 1958 and submitted its report in December 1960 to the Ministry of Home Affairs.
4. *Committee on Customary Rights* (C.C.) : The Central Department of Social Welfare appointed a committee in 1965 under the chairmanship of Prof. N.R. Malkani to examine the question of the abolition of customary rights of the scavengers. The committee submitted its report to the Government in 1966.
5. *Pandya Committee* (P.C.) : The National Commission of Labour constituted by the Union Ministry of Labour appointed a sub-committee (1968-69) under the chairmanship of Shri Bhanu Prasad Pandya to look into the working and service conditions of the scavengers.

The recommendations of above-mentioned committees and commissions are listed below :

1. General Awareness about the Scavenger Community

1. Various processes of scavenging problem such as use of defective and good latrine, methods of scavenging, working at pail-depots, dumping grounds and system of carriage etc., can be filmed by the Ministry of Information and Broadcasting in consultation with the Ministry of Home Affairs and the good and bad spots in the country presented before the masses who should be educated in the use of improved methods. (M.C.)
2. The documentaries, cinema slides etc., prepared by the Films Division of the Ministry of Information and Broadcasting, would be of great help in creating opinion for improving the conditions of scavenging and those of scavengers. (M.C.)

3. The Ministry of Home Affairs and the State Governments/ Union Administrations should ensure that those non-official organisations who get financial assistance either from the Centre or the State Government must include scheme for the improvement of the conditions of scavenging and scavengers in their programmes. They should be asked to publish posters, leaflets etc., propagating the need for improvement of the conditions. The organisations who have got cinema vans should be asked to make use of such vans for the purpose of schemes for putting an end to the practice of carrying nightsoil as head-loads. (M.C.)
4. The sanitary conscience, civic sense and the sense of social justice of the people should be aroused by impressing upon them the importance of public sanitation and improved sanitary arrangements in their own dwellings. (B.C.)

2. Living Conditions

1. The scavengers should not be condemned to live in segregated localities. They should be distributed and given quarters among other groups. (K.K.C.)
2. Quarters for conservancy staff should be as near their place of work as possible but never around the pail-depots, morgues, public latrines, dumping grounds, etc. Location of scavengers' quarters at such places amounts to criminal neglect. A few quarters here and a few there may be built in colonies inhabited by others as well to avoid segregation and give an impression of a mixed colony. (B.C. & M.C.)
3. It is of primary importance that the housing conditions of scavengers are radically improved. This would create a new sense of self-respect in them and particularly in their children. (M.C.)
4. For the welfare of scavengers, maximum use of the slum clearance schemes should be made. It is necessary to have a special provision in the plan under the Works and Housing Ministry for providing houses to the conservancy staff of the local bodies. (M.C.)

5. One-room tenements are not adequate. Scavengers have large families and even taking an average of five members per family, one-room tenements are too small. From the point of view of moral hygiene also every tenement must make provision for two living rooms, a kitchen, a bathroom, a latrine flushout or any other sanitary type like septic tank etc. Wherever possible, electricity must also be provided. Water supply is a necessity. (M.C.)
6. It is very important that amenities like primary school, a welfare centre with a community hall which may be used as a community centre, medical facilities, etc., are provided in large colonies. A social worker should invariably be provided to be in-charge of the welfare activities. There is a need for appointing a social worker for covering a population of 100 families. (B.C. & M.C.)
7. Creches should be started in the colonies of scavengers where a paid worker preferably a trained lady worker may be appointed to look after the children. Children must be taught clean ways of living and habits so as to make them clean persons. (M.C.)
8. State Governments and local bodies should ensure that children of scavengers are provided easy admissions in schools and hostels irrespective of their caste. Efforts should be made to open primary schools near their bastis where children of scavengers and other communities may receive education. (M.C.)
9. All the State Governments etc. should conduct a medical survey and find out if the scavengers suffer from any disease due to handling nightsoil. If so, proper medical arrangements for them should be made. Scavengers must at least be examined periodically. (M.C.)
10. There should be established community centres where care of children is combined with training of women in some crafts and adult education. Such community centres should also be used for cultural purposes and amusements etc. (M.C.)
11. Rearing of pigs in any area of towns must not be allowed. If

anybody wants to rear piggery he should do so on the proper lines away from towns. (M.C.)

12. House rent should be paid to all scavengers who have neither a house of their own nor have been provided free accommodation by local bodies. (B.C.)
13. A campaign must be planned by the Public Health authorities of states, with the cooperation of local bodies and social workers for the purpose of securing improvements in the living condition of the scavengers and generally for the upliftment of scavengers as members of society. (B.C.)

3. Working Conditions

The Receptacle

1. The use of receptacles in private and public latrines should be made compulsory. (M.C.)
2. The non-use of receptacles in latrines should be made an offence and the defaulters dealt with properly. (M.C.)
3. The house-owners left to themselves would not go in for the receptacles even though it is made obligatory and penalty imposed for failure to provide the receptacles. The receptacles should therefore, be supplied periodically, at least once a year or so if the first is broken or damaged, by the local body directly or through licensed shops on a no-profit no-loss basis, and if necessary at subsidised rates. (M.C.)
4. It should be the duty of the scavenger and the area sanitary inspector to report to the local body about a receptacle which might be broken or damaged. (M.C.)
5. The number of public latrines should conform to the demand for them in the area on the basis of their usage. It is desirable to prescribe a standard proportion to the population of the area and conform to it. (M.C.)
6. As far as possible, all public buildings like offices, schools,

hospitals etc, should have flushout latrines failing which septic tank latrines or aqua privies be provided. But where this is not possible, it should be ensured that standardised receptacles are provided. (M.C. & B.C.)

7. Wherever new buildings, colonies or townships are built by Government or with Government aid or by local bodies and in all industrial housing programmes, the latrines must be of sanitary type. (M.C. & B.C.)

The Scraper

1. It should be obligatory to use a standardised scraper which should be supplied by the local bodies to their employees and not left to the scavengers themselves. (M.C.)
2. In case of private scavengers, the local bodies should supply the standardised scraper directly or through licensed dealers at no-profit no-loss basis and it should be made obligatory to use such a scraper. (M.C.)

The Rubber Gloves

1. Efforts should be made to encourage the use of rubber gloves particularly at the pail-depots and dumping grounds. (M.C.)

The Head-Load

1. Carrying of nightsoil in basket, *tasla* and drum etc., as head-load should be prohibited by law and made an offence. (M.C. & B.C.)
2. For stopping carrying of nightsoil as head-load, persuasive methods should also be adopted and they can be more effective than legislation. (M.C. & B.C.)

The Bucket

1. In the narrow lanes which are unpaved or have ups and

downs, wheel-barrows cannot ply conveniently and cannot be taken right up to the latrine seat. For such cases, there is no alternative but to introduce buckets. The bucket when full can be carried to the wheel-barrow standing nearby. (M.C.)

2. Private scavengers should also be compelled to use small covered buckets which can be supplied to them by the local bodies on no-profit no-loss basis. (B.C.)
3. The broken or damaged buckets should be replaced immediately. (M.C.)

The Cess-Pools

1. Collection of nightsoil in cess-pools is most insanitary and inhuman use of scavengers engaged in cleaning them should be stopped. (M.C.)
2. The contents of cess-pools must not be carried as head-load. (M.C.)
3. Cess-pools maintained by the local bodies, particularly those attached to public latrines, should not be allowed to continue. All the pail-depots where nightsoil is collected in big drums should be closed down. (M.C.)
4. Abolition of cess-pools in private houses is likely to take some time. As long as these are in existence, the local bodies must introduce mechanical devices for cleaning them periodically. There should be a suction system. (M.C. & B.C.)
5. Corporations or big municipalities or such local bodies as may afford, should think seriously in terms of introducing vacuum cars/lorries etc., as used in Japan for cleansing cess-pools. (M.C.)

Washing of Latrines

1. It should be ensured that latrines are washed properly and regularly. (M.C. & B.C.)
2. The scavengers should be given access to latrines. (M.C.)

Transportation of Nightsoil

1. After collection, nightsoil is taken in basket, *tasla*, drum etc., either as head or waist-load to the pail-depot, carriage van or the place of disposal. This is most inhuman. The entire process of carrying nightsoil as head-load or waist-load, which is the root cause of all the troubles, has to be revolutionised. (M.C. & B.C.)
2. For putting an end to the practice of carrying nightsoil as head-load or waist-load, wheel-barrows should be introduced. (M.C.& B.C.)
3. The man-drawn carts for carrying nightsoil are an insult to human dignity and must be abolished. (M.C. & B.C.)
4. The local bodies should introduce improved types of nightsoil vans, tankers and trailers. (M.C. & B.C.)
5. Some local bodies collect nightsoil in overhead tanks or big drums which have to be emptied into nightsoil vans for transportation. In some places, nightsoil is churned and collected in pools before transportation. Such storage tanks and churning operations must not be allowed to continue. (M.C.)
6. The nightsoil barrels used for collection purpose should be placed at higher levels so that nightsoil can be poured out right into the nightsoil lorry tanker, or better still there should be a suction system. (M.C.)

Wheel-Barrows

1. The crude type of wheel-barrows already in use in some states should be discarded. (M.C.)
2. The frame of wheel-barrow should be all steel one with solid rubber tyre wheels with ball bearings. There should be two pails in the wheel-barrows. The pails should not be of more than 5 gallons capacity each and the combined capacity of 8 gallons when full. The lids of the pails should be collapsible and fixed with hinges to the body of the pails.

The bottom of the pail should be such that nightsoil does not stick. (M.C.)

3. Even women scavengers would not resist the use of such light wheel-barrows. At some places, women have already taken to wheel-barrows. (M.C.)
4. The manufacture of the proposed type of wheel-barrows on a large scale to meet requirements throughout the state could be centralised to some place for distribution to all local bodies in which case the cost of wheel-barrow would definitely come further down and the design will conform to the required pattern uniformly. (M.C.)
5. Wherever necessary, some administrative adjustments may be carried out. Men may do the pushing and women the cleaning. The wheel-barrows may be kept moving from house to house along with the women workers. (M.C.)
6. The main difficulty in popularising the introduction of wheel-barrows is the passive attitude of scavengers. This requires tactful handling. The local authorities should make a beginning with a few intelligent scavengers and with the assistance of non-official organisations and social workers, persuade scavengers to use wheel-barrows. (M.C.)
7. The Public Health Officers can by persuasion and by amending the bye-laws etc., achieve substantial measure of success. (M.C.)
8. The number of wheel-barrows can be reduced with the extension of the underground drainage line. (M.C.)
9. The trailers must be placed at places within easy approach of scavengers and where these are needed more. (M.C.)

Nightsoil Depots

1. The existing conditions of the nightsoil pail-depots and the scavengers working there are extremely unsatisfactory and deserve immediate attention of local bodies. (M.C.)
2. The number of pail-depots must be increased according to the needs. The pail-depots should be constructed at places

where it is convenient and within easy reach of the scavengers. (M.C.)

3. Cess-pools for storing nightsoil before transportation should not be allowed to continue. (M.C.)
4. The workers at nightsoil depots must be provided with gum-boots, gloves, aprons, waterproof headgears, long spades and rakes etc., for pulling out cloth pieces etc. to avoid clogging. (M.C.)
5. The structure of such depots where perforce the scavengers have to wade through nightsoil must be altered. Provision of trailers can minimise the difficulty to a great extent. (M.C.)
6. At every pail-depot, there must be an attendant. It should be his duty to handle the load at the depot. (M.C.)

Amenities at Pail-Depots

1. At every pail-depot arrangements for the supply of sufficient water for washing the vehicles, wheel-barrows, drums, the depot etc. clothes must be provided. (M.C.)
2. There may be separate bathrooms for men and women. A set for each can be sufficient in most of the cases. The number may be increased if necessary. (M.C.)
3. Where possible, arrangements for changing clothes before and after the work should be made. (M.C.)

Hours of Work

1. For full-time employees, the hours of work should not be more than 7 hours per day of which only 4 to 5 hours may be reserved for scavenging work. Part-time workers should not be asked to work both in the morning and evening as this deprives them of any other work and causes them hardships. (B.C. & M.C.)

Roll Call

1. The scavengers on duty should be called only twice for roll

call once in the morning and once in the afternoon. (M.C.)

Leave Rules

1. Local bodies should frame leave rules and the scavengers should be given the benefit of casual, privilege, earned leave etc. (M.C.)
2. Women scavengers must be given pre-natal and post-natal leave. They should be given leave in case of miscarriage etc., also. (M.C.)

Off Day in a Week

1. State Governments/Union Administrations should see that at least in local bodies the scavengers are allowed a full day off in a week. (B.C. & M.C.)

Uniforms

1. All the local bodies should give sufficient and proper summer and winter uniforms both to male and female scavengers. (M.C.)
2. Proper kit for scavengers for cleaning underground drains should be supplied. (B.C. & M.C.)

Permanency of Service

1. Every effort should be made by the local bodies to give some security of employment to the temporary scavengers and avoid keeping them on a temporary basis for an indefinite period. (M.C.)

Full-time and Part-time Workers

1. Local bodies as far as possible should not appoint part-time scavengers. Full-time worker is bound to be more efficient. (M.C.)

4. Customary Rights

1. Private scavengers have customary rights not only for cleaning latrines in certain localities but at some places over the possession and disposal of nightsoil also. Such customary rights must not in any case be allowed to continue and be abrogated immediately. (B.C. & M.C.)
2. The local bodies should pay reasonable compensation in cash to such scavengers who might be affected and do not get employment due to abrogation of customary rights. (M.C.)
3. The governments at the centre and state should come forward to finance such of the local bodies which are not in a position to pay reasonable compensation. (M.C.)
4. Wherever cash compensation is not possible, or the local bodies cannot offer employment under them, the affected scavengers would be prepared to forgo their customary rights if provided with municipal services. (M.C.)
5. The Malkani Committee pointed out that the scavengers doing cleaning work in private households either on their own or under the employment of some other scavengers have come to possess these rights according to which they rctain, sell or mortgage the rights in the same manner as one does with his property. The committee recommended compensation for loss of customary rights either in cash, or by employment in the municipal services. (M.C.)
6. The committee found that where scavengers are not municipalised and latrines are cleaned privately, one particular scavenger acquires hereditary right to clean such laterines as against another scavenger, by a tacit understanding and agreement. A customary relationship also develops with the householder and the scavenger receives payments in some form or other.

   In small towns he is generally paid in kind (a daily *roti*) and some perquisites like food or clothes etc. on some special occasions like births, marriage, deaths, etc. Varying with the status of the householder often in bigger towns he is also paid partially in cash by each family served by him and in cities is generally paid only in cash. The households are unable to change the scavengers when desired. But a scavenger may enter into a deal with another on payment of an amount according to the status of the household.

There have been cases of mortgage but sales are stated to be rare. However, the committee did not consider these rights to have the essential character of valid custom, nor could such rights be enforced in court of law. In fact, the High Courts of Allahabad and Madhya Pradesh have ruled against the enforcement of such a right. As regards the right to undertake the disposal of nightsoil, it is only in Punjab that Section 54-B of the Municipal Act, 1911 seems to indicate that propriety of the task of removal of nightsoil may rest in a person other than the Municipality and that the Municipality may acquire this right on payment of some compensation. (B.C., M.C. & C.C.)

7. All the same, the committee felt that in recognition of the services rendered by scavengers and their forefathers, some sort of compensation or relief or exgratia grant would appear to be necessary and reasonable. The question was, however, largely seen by the committee in the light of its proposal for municipalisation of the services and it was expected that the private scavengers would be offered employment or some compensation. But in the event of conversion of dry latrine into a water seal one, the whole business of removal of nightsoil by another scavenger or by the municipality disappears. The weak customary right becomes practically extinct. No compensation has been paid for the conversion of latrines in a number of cities and towns in Madhya Pradesh but the social reform activities of the Harijan Sevak Sangh have helped in the change of occupation. The problem, however, is different, where the municipal agency employs a contigent of scavengers, who cannot be retrenched just because there are no latrines to be serviced. (C.C.)

8. The committee are strongly of the opinion that the Gharki

System or the system of customary right of scavengers should be abolished both in the interest of the Bhangis and also in the interest of public sanitation. The latter reason has arisen because Bhangis who had customary right had the upperhand over the residents of towns and villages because they would do the cleansing work only as and when they pleased and at the same time they would not allow other scavengers to enter into their sphere of work to carry on the work in case of strikes etc. This leads to a high degree of insanitation in many cases. (B.C.)

5. Remuneration for Wages and other Financial Aspects

1. Wages would be paid to scavengers according to the Minimum Wages Act. (M.C.)
2. The State Government and Union Administrations, who have not done it so far, must appoint small committees to go into the whole question of wages and payment of other allowances to scavengers and suggest basic wages which should, however, not fall below the minimum wages. Question of payment of other allowances as may be admissible to scavengers must also be considered. (M.C.)
3. Unclean Work Allowance should not be in cash but in the form of extra amenities such as gloves, water etc., to make the occupation more clean. Extra allowance paid in cash is not utilised properly and the work remains unclean. Such a terminology should not be used. Unclean work allowance can very well be called like any other ordinary allowance.
4. For administration of various schemes, the main burden will have to be borne by the local bodies concerned with or without the assistance from the State Government. They will have to make necessary adjustments and provisions in their bye-laws, rules etc. (M.C.)
5. For purchase of wheel-barrows, the local bodies find it difficult to find out adequate financial resources. The best course would be for the Government of India to meet the

entire cost towards the purchase of wheel-barrows; failing which:

(a) The poorest local bodies should be given 100 per cent assistance—75 per cent to be given by the Central Government and 25 per cent by the State Governments—the entire amount to be treated as grant;

(b) For medium local bodies, the government grant can be 75 per cent—50 per cent to be given by the Central Government and 25 per cent by the State Governments and the local body to contribute only the remaining 25 per cent from its own resources; and

(c) For the bigger municipalities and corporations etc., the Government of India's assistance should be 50 per cent, the rest to be borne by the local body alone or by the local body and State Government concerned together. (M.C.)

6. In all the cases where the local bodies concerned need loans for meeting their share of expenditure, the State Government should help the local bodies by advancing loans to them. (M.C.)
7. For purchase of other mechanical equipments like tractors and trailers or vans etc., the State Governments should find the fund which may be advanced to the local bodies as grants wherever possible or otherwise in the form of loans. If possibile, necessary funds may also be found from the agricultural programmes for converting nightsoil into manure. If the Ministry of Health provides any funds for such purpose that may be made use of. (M.C.)
8. A specific amount must be earmarked for the underground drainage schemes separately and at least 3.33 per cent of the total allocations for the National Water Supply and Drainage Schemes shou'd be earmarked for drainage schemes. (M.C.)

9. The local bodies may examine the possibility of allowing some rebate in house, latrine tax etc., to such of the parties who may like to convert their dry latrines into water-borne etc. (M.C.)

Co-operative Societies

1. The local authorities may consider the possibilities of establishing cooperative societies for the purchase and sale of compost. (M.C.)

6. Administrative Arrangements and Legislation

1. The problem of improving the scavenging conditions should be dealt with by the Local Self Government Departments of the States/Union Administrations or such other departments as may be concerned with it. (M.C.)
2. The State Government/Union Administration should appoint special officers exclusively to look after the problems of scavenging and scavengers. (M.C.)
3. The Central Government must appoint an officer having the necessary background knowledge of the various problems of scavenging and scavengers in the country at the centre to deal with these problems and watch their day-to-day development. (M.C.)
4. A small vigilance committee consisting of non-officials, who are well-acquainted with the magnitude of the problem and have shown serious interest in tackling it, should be appointed by the Ministry of Home Affairs to move from State to State, meet and discuss with officials, social workers and members of the public about the urgency of the problem and mobilise their efforts for solving it. (M.C.)
5. The Ministry of Home Affairs which is concerned with the Welfare of Scheduled Castes should initiate legislation for the abolition of customary rights, if necessary. (M.C.)
6. The State Government/Union Administration should explore possibility of framing rules, bye-laws etc., which they may

consider necessary for the solution of various problems. (M.C.)

7. Government should appoint an assistant to each Director of local authorities in a State in order to secure the implementation of the committee's recommendations. (M.C.)

7. Some General Aspects

1. Latrines should be introduced in villages also progressively and people must stop the present indecent and insanitary practice of easing everywhere. It is indecent to observe a large number of people squatting all along the railway lines etc. (M.C.)
2. The committee have suggested that the nightsoil should be used for the production of gas for street lighting, fuel, etc. There are gas plants already manufactured in the country which can be used for this purpose. Public latrines should be so constructed that the nightsoil etc., should enter special tank built for the plant from which gas will be produced and after the gas bas been yielded the residue would still retain its manurial value. (B.C.)
3. If as a result of improvement in the conditions of work of the scavengers as mentioned above, some of them are thrown out of employment, it should be the duty of the local bodies to see that such persons are absorbed in other suitable kind of employment under their control. (B.C.)
4. Local bodies, Gram Panchayats and other local authorities should include in their annual reports a special chapter giving details about living conditions and the conditions of work of scavengers and sweepers in their employ and the improvements effected therein during the year under review. (B.C.)
5. Co-operative Credit Societies should be organised with the help of local bodies for the use of the servants of local bodies including scavengers. (B.C.)

8

WOMEN SCAVENGERS

Scavenging is a profession with a difference. It is evident in the system of payment and above all in gender involvement. Among the scavengers men and women share work in and outside the house. They do have some division of labour among themselves as far as household work is concerned. But this has now changed. Personal ability to earn determines their role and performance. Previously men used to help in household tasks only when women were sick or otherwise physically not in a condition to work. But now if the female is working, the domestic work of the family is equally shared by the male family members.

In the scavenger community, it has been noticed that women earn more than men. Women outnumber men in the Municipal Corporation/Nigam. Apart from that they have more secondary occupation options as house-maid. The economic strength of women in this community makes them more important in the family. To meet the personal and family expenses men are almost dependent on women. This dependency also leads to men sharing in different kinds of domestic work.

Male members in the scavenger community are quite active in house work and child care. Scavenger women go back to work soon after giving birth, particularly after the second or later birth. They sometimes take young babies out with them at the place of work. Since in the urban area most of the scavengers are from nuclear family, in most of the cases the father has to bear the responsibility of child care.

It has been noticed that in urban areas women in the scavenger community are very fond of periodical purchase of new dresses for themselves and their children along with other consumer items.

Another dimension of gender perspective is that while men are increasingly leaving the highly 'defiling' occupation of their caste, women continue in the traditional field. These women have to support the males of the household who are trying to acquire skills for entering new occupations, or exploring independent source of income. The men, even when unemployed, are loath to touch their traditional work. Boys are sent to school while girls join their mothers at work at an early age. Thus, women contribute to occupational continuity within the parameters of the patrilineal system and under the control of the caste organisation.

The status of women in the scavenger community is comparatively higher than among other such communities. This directly affects the male hegemony. Women, due to their earning ability, are free to remarry if the situation demands. Despite the fact that women in the scavenger community enjoys a lot of authority and respect, the attitude towards educating the girl child is still negative. Most of them are of the opinion that there is no need to waste money on girls' education. It will not only keep them away from work but at the same time their marriage will become a problem. Among the scavengers, at the time of marriage education of the girl is not regarded as a qualification. It is a disqualification as an educated partner has to be found for her and this is an expensive affair.

Women in this community are free to spend their self-earned money. It has been noticed that in urban area women in the scavenger community purchase new dresses for themselves and their children along with other consumer items. This has also encouraged conspicuous consumption among the women. In this may be included expenses on drinking and gambling.

Head-loading is still in practice and most of the head-loaders are women. Despite all the efforts by the Government and the NGOs this curse is still in practice and it certainly marginalises the status of women scavengers in and outside the community. It has been noticed that the main reason behind this problem is lack of occupational mobility and awareness.

The cultural recognition of the significance of women's work in the continuity of caste-linked occupation is clear. At the same time, in order that women pursue these traditional occupations, they have to be trained in them from childhood and have to be socialised into accepting them as proper work which, within limits, is 'destiny'. It has been found that parents may restrict the education of girls to avoid a potentially uncomfortable situation in which the daughter develops an aversion for the traditional occupation of her caste. Not formal education, but the capacity and willingness to do traditional work tends to make a girl useful in the husband's family.

Table 8.1: Freedom in Spending Self-Earned Income

Area	Yes	No	No Response	Total
Urban	82.70%	72.78%	100%	80.91%
Rural	17.29%	27.21%	00%	19.08%
Total	67.88%	26.97%	5.13%	100%

Table 8.1 reveals that in the urban area about 69.38% respondents in the female category were at liberty to spend their earned money. Among the scavengers, earning of money irrespective of sex is considered a vital issue. More earning generates more prosperity in the family, thus raising the quality of life. Scavenger women who have almost equal opportunity to earn always capitalise this advantage. This income has made them able to pull their weight in family decision-making. Now she realises that she can happily remarry or can stay alone if her husband deserts her for some reason.

Table 8.2 shows that almost 92.20% women respondents were of the opinion that they were consulted on important family issues. In the urban area 92.51% respondents were consulted on vital issues whereas in the rural areas 90.86% respondents had this privilege. In the urban area 54.41% respondents who are consulted on vital issues belong to the income group of Rs. 2001 to 4000 whereas, in the rural area the maximum concentration (72.48%) of respondents is in the income group of below Rs. 2000.

Women's participation in crafting household decisions is gradually increasing in the scavenger community. Most of the

Table 8.2: Women's Share in Dealing with Vital Issues

Income Group	Urban		Rural		Total	
	Yes	No	Yes	No	Yes	No
Below 2000	22.67%	19.69%	72.48%	68.42%	32.03%	30.58%
2001 to 4000	54.41%	65.15%	27.51%	31.57%	49.35%	57.64%
4001 to 6000	21.93%	15.15%	0.00%	0.00%	17.81%	11.73%
Above 6000	0.98%	0.00%	0.00%	0.00%	0.79%	0.00%
Total	92.51%	7.48%	90.86%	9.13%	92.20%	7.79%
Grand Total	80.91%	0.00%	19.08%	0.00%	100%	0.00%

marriages are finalised by the women members of the family. Issues pertaining to education are also in most of the cases decided by the women.

Table 8.3: Head-loading

Area	Yes	No	Total
Urban	2.61%	90.15%	80.92%
Rural	97.39%	9.85%	19.08%
Total	10.55%	89.45%	100%

Table 8.3 reveals that 10.55% respondents were of the opinion that head-loading had decreased in past decades. 2.61% urban respondents and 97.39% rural respondents were of this view.

The general perception that head-loading has decreased in the urban area in comparison to rural area is incorrect. In the urban area according to the respondents head-loading has not decreased. Migration and occupation mobility on the other land have produced a sea-change in the rural area where head-loading has almost ended.

Table 8.4 reveals the reasons for taking up the profession of head-loading by the female respondents. About 44.31% of the women respondents were of the opinion that this is their hereditary profession. Among those who inherited this profession about 81.37%

Table 8.4: Table Showing Reasons for Entering this Profession

Reason	Urban	Rural	All
Tradition	81.37	18.63	100.00
	44.55	43.27	44.31
Economic	80.33	19.67	100.00
	54.65	56.73	55.05
Any Other	100.00	0.00	100.00
	0.80	0.00	0.64
Total	81.00	19.00	100%
	100.00	100.00	100.00

respondents reside in urban area and 18.63% respondents in the rural area. Pursuing this profession due to economic gain has been advanced by 55.05% respondents, 80.33% in urban and 19.67% in rural area.

The traditional view on head-loading is no more rigid and it has been noticed that those who wanted to get rid of this had been successful in their endeavour. Lack of other professional avenues has definitely forced some of them to continue this inhuman practice. As this caste has a monopoly of this profession, it easily suits them in the absence of other alternative to make a living.

Table 8.5: Misbehaviour Experienced at the Work Place

Area	Yes	No	No Response	Total
Urban	53.17%	44.10%	2.72%	
	79.90%	81.21%	100%	80.92%
Rural	56.73%	43.27%	0.00%	
	20.10%	18.79%	0.00%	19.08%
Grand Total	53.85%	43.95%	2.20%	100%

Table 8.5 shows that 53.85% respondents have reported that they have experienced misbehaviour from men during working hours. 79.90% respondents reside in urban area and 20.10% in rural

area.

The misbehaviour with scavenger women is not only confined to places where they go for work. They are sometimes subjected to sexual exploitation by the lower municipal staff. Those who are working in private houses are also equally vulnerable. In certain situations if they try to resist, they generally lose their job.

In some incidents of misbehaviour at work place, women have started showing protest. The menfolk do not join them during such crisis movements and it is left to the women to fight on their own. In rural areas sometimes jati panchayat is also summoned. Role of formal agencies like police is not effective.

Summing Up

The overall status of women scavengers has been raised due to increase in their earning ability. This factor has elevated their importance in the decision-making of the family as well.

Male members of the scavenger community are not shy of performing domestic work like cooking and child care. This shift in the division of labour can be attributed to more outdoor working of the females.

Right to spend the earned money among the females is gaining a firm ground in this community but at the same time it has led to an increase in undesirable expenditure like drinking etc. It has enhanced their ability to meet expenditure to promote better living. Misbehaviour with the females at the work place still continues and no substantial remedial mechanism has been evolved as yet.

In urban areas, head-loading has not decreased despite lot of hue and cry. This system has marginalised the status of female members of this community. It also shows lack of occupational mobility among the female scavengers. In the absence of other suitable jobs and due to economic necessity, the females are left with no other option but to continue the profession in which their community had a monopoly.

On the whole it seems that whatever prosperity the women in this community have achieved is only due to their own personal efforts and not due to Government-sponsored action.

9

IMPACT OF WELFARE PROGRAMMES

Scavengers have been the victims of institutionalisd oppression of the traditional Hindu society. The issue of the emancipation of the scavengers is in fact tied up with the caste system.

There have been several attempts at ameliorating the lot of scavengers. Arya Samaj, Prarthana Samaj, Brahma Samaj, Keshav Chandra Sen, Mahatma Gandhi, Dayanand Saraswati, Swami Vivekanand and All India Harijan Sevak Sangh initiated socio-economic reform among them and condemned untouchability but this community could not get a fair deal. The liberation of scavengers has remained a problem.

After independence the government of free India paid attention to this problem. In 1953 the Backward Classes Commission was set up by the Ministry of Home Affairs. The Commission observed that the hand collection and hand carriage of nightsoil should be obviated by mechanical cleaning of latrines and provision of sewers, drains etc., on a large scale. Training in cleanliness and hygiene and provision of better housing would improve their living standard and help their integration with the larger society. A similar approach was suggested by the Scavenging Conditions Enquiry Committee.

The Malkani Committee (1960) observed "As long as dry latrines continue, the problem will exist and it is a story of the far distant future to think of all the towns having underground sewers". The problem of scavengers was also examined by the various working groups constituted by the Planning Commission for the development of scheduled castes and tribes during successive Five-year Plans. The main recommendation of all these working groups was that a time-bound programme should be taken up to convert all the dry latrines in the country within a period of four to five years.

In 1958-59 a centrally sponsored scheme of improvement in the working and living conditions of those engaged in unclean occupations was introduced. Under the scheme, grant-in-aid was given to the municipalities/local bodies for the purchase of handcarts, wheel-barrows, scrappers, gumboots and other protective devices, similar efforts were also made in 1967, 1968 and 1975. Despite these efforts, manual scavenging remains in practice as is evident from the available data on dry latrines in 1989 in Bihar. It was estimated that about 14,32,934 and 1,01,48,311 dry latrines exist in urban and rural areas respectively.

Along with the scheme of dry latrine conversion, the training scheme and financial assistance under rehabilitation programme also gave impetus for the overall development of the scavengers. Some of them are as follows:

(A) National Scheduled Castes and Scheduled Tribes Finance and Development Corporation (NSFDC)

The NSFDC was established on 8th February 1989 as a semi-Government organisation. The focus of NSFDC is on the special development and financing needs (loan only) of the SCs and STs over the above the credit available through priority sector lendings of banks and other institutions. NSFDC provides financial assistance at concessional rates for income generating activities and training in skill development to SCs and STs whose annual income is below double the poverty line criteria *i.e.* Rs. 22,000 per annum in rural areas and Rs. 23,700 per annum in urban areas. The asistance is provided through the various States Scheduled Caste Development Corporations (SCDCs) and other State Channelising Agencies (SCAs) for implementing technically feasible and financially viable schemes/projects besides providing grants for skill development programmes organised by SCAs and non-Government Organisations (NGOs).

In Bihar, NSFDC targeted 4,000 scavengers for training and rehabitation in the year 1997-98, out of which only 536 were trained and 72 were rehabilitated. Rs. 6.1 lakh was provided as subsidy and

Rs. 2.53 lakh as margin money under this scheme.

(B) National Scheme of Liberation and Rehabilitation of Scavengers and their Dependants

The National Scheme of Liberation and Rehabilitation of Scavengers and their Dependants was launched by the Government of India in March 1992, in pursuance of the commitment to eliminate the inhuman practice of manual handling of nighsoil and filth by the end of Eighth Plan period, with the following three components :

(i) A periodical survey to identify scavengers and their dependance and their aptitude for alternative trades and professions.
(ii) Training of scavengers and their dependants.
(iii) Rehabilitation of scavengers through projects with a prescribed funding pattern.

The implementation of the scheme at the grass-root level is looked after by the SCDCs. The National Scheduled Castes and Scheduled Tribes Finance and Development Corporation (NSFDC) has been entrusted with the responsibility of day-to-day implementation and monitoring of the scheme as well as coordination and collaboration with the SCDCs in implementing the scheme. The overall implementation of the scheme has been entrusted to the District Collectors/Deputy Commissioners. Training is imparted through the existing institutes of the Central Govt. and Semi-Govt. Organisations.

There is a prescribed financial package for rehabilitation of scavengers in alternative trades through provision of financial assistance upto Rs. 50,000 per beneficiary. This includes a subsidy of 50% of the capital cost subject to a ceiling of Rs.10,000 per project, margin money loan of 15% of the project cost at 4% rate of interest, and the remaining portion by way of loan finance to be provided by commercial banks.

The progress of the scheme is being monitored and frequently reviewed by the Government of India. Its effective implementation has begun only from 1993-94. The progress registered by most of the states has been tardy except the state of Madhya Pradesh as given in the table about statewise utilization of funds from 1991 to 1999. The major problems which impeded effective implementation of the scheme were : (i) inadequate stipend given for training, (ii) delay in transfer of funds by the State Governments to SCDCs, (iii) unviable projects taken up for rehabilitation of scavengers, (iv) reluctance of banks to finance projects under the scheme, (v) weak infrastructure at grass-root level, and (vi) lack of coordination between the schemes implemented by the Ministry of Urban Affairs and the Ministry of Welfare.

In Bihar, since the inception of this programme, none of the scavenger family got the benefit of this scheme.

(C) National Safai Karamchari Finance and Development Corporation (NSKFDC)

The Cabinet has approved the setting up of the National Safai Karamchari Finance and Development Corporation under Section 25 of the Companies Act, 1956 with its registered office at Delhi, having an authorised share capital of Rs. 200 crores. The major objectives for setting up a separate Financial Corporation for safai karamcharis are to promote economic development/self-employment for the economic rehabilitation of safai karamcharis besides providing training in technical and entrepreneurial skills and extending loans to students from safai karamcharis community for pursuing higher education. The NSKFDC will function as an apex institution for channelising funds through the State Channelising Agencies authorised by the State Govts./U.T. Administrations. The NSKFDC will also coordinate and monitor the schemes/programmes implemented through authorised State Finance and Development Corporations/Boards/UT Administrations financed by the Corporation.

Under the National Scheme of Liberation and Rehabilitation of Scavengers and Their Dependants, Bihar received Rs. 3.50 crores in the financial year 1991-92. It was followed with the sanction of Rs. 3.13 crores and 4.64 crores in the financial year 1992-93 and

1997-98 respectively (*Source*: Ministry of Welfare Annual Report, Government of India, 1997-98). Despite this fund availability the official figure shows that out of the 40,249 scavengers in the State none of them and their dependants were liberated and rehabilitated (Ministry of Welfare Annual Report, Government of India, 1997-98).

Two NGOs *viz*., Ambedkar Institute for Research and Rehabilitation and Sulabh Institute for Research and Rehabilitation, are involved in imparting training to scavengers in different trades. The latter is also involved in the rehabilitation work. Sulabh has till date trained 3,000 scavenger children in different trades.

(D) Bihar State Scheduled Caste Cooperative Development Corporation

This agency works for the socio-economic upliftment of the scheduled castes. There are many schemes under which this Corporation provides training and financial loan. For the scavengers there is specific scheme called GARIMA for providing them an alternative opportunity for selecting an occupation. This scheme covers all family members of a household. Under this scheme there is a provision of six months' training with a stipend of Rs. 150 per month. The selection of the beneficiary and his training is conducted at district level.

Table 9.1: List of GARIMA Scheme beneficiaries

Name of District	No. of Trainees	Years
Deoghar	50	1996-97
Munger	236	1995-97
Bhojpur	20	1995-97
Gaya	149	1995-97
Bhagalpur	41	1995-96
Gopalganj	20	1995-96
Vaishali	20	1995-96

(Contd.)

Table 9.1: *(Contd.)*

Patna	275	1991-98
Darbhanga	77	1995-96
Muzaffarpur	31	1995-96
Begusarai	16	1995-96
Madhubani	11	1995-96
Saran	10	1995-96
Siwan	12	1995-96
Jamui	32	1998-99

Tables concerning the knowledge of different welfare schemes and the benefits of the schemes in relation to different categories are discussed below.

Table 9.2: Table showing information regarding Government Welfare Schemes among the Respondents

	Urban			Rural			All		
	Male	Female	Total	Male	Female	Total	Male	Female	Total
	57.07	42.93	100%	63.27	36.73	100%	57.53	42.47	100%
Yes	355	267	622	31	18	49	386	285	671
	31.75	30.27	31.00	12.81	8.65	11.00	28.38	26.15	27.00
	55.37	44.63	100%	52.62	47.38	100%	54.75	45.25	100%
No	763	615	1378	211	190	401	974	805	1779
	68.25	69.73	69.00	87.19	91.35	89.00	71.62	73.85	73.00
	55.9	44.1	100%	54.00	46.0	100%	56.60	44.0	100%
All	1118	882	2000	242	208	450	1360	1090	2450
	100%	100%	100%	100%	100%	100%	100%	100%	100%

Table 9.2 shows the awareness among scavengers regarding Government Welfare Schemes, viz. Education, Minimum Needs Programmes, Housing, Old Age Pension, Availability of Mechanical Tools, Loan and Training and Rehabilitation Schemes. Only 27% respondents were aware about the different Government Welfare Schemes. Out of these 57.33% respondents are male. About 93%

Table 9.3: Table Showing Source of Information Regarding Government Welfare Schemes

	Urban			Rural			All		
	Male	Female	Total	Male	Female	Total	Male	Female	Total
Politicians	50.00	50.00	100%	75.00	25.00	100%	50.91	49.09	100%
	7.32	9.74	8.36	6.45	5.56	6.12	7.25	9.47	8.20
N.G.O.	60.00	40.00	100%	60.00	40.00	100%	60.00	40.00	100%
	0.84	0.75	0.80	9.68	11.11	10.20	1.55	1.40	1.49
Govt.	27.27	72.73	100%	55.56	44.44	100%	44.83	55.17	100%
	0.84	3.00	1.77	32.26	44.44	36.73	3.37	5.61	4.32
T.V.	61.19	38.81	100%	0.00	0.00	0.00	61.19	38.81	100%
	11.55	9.74	10.77	0.00	0.00	0.00	10.62	9.12	9.98
Newspaper	78.20	21.80	100%	100.00	0.00	100%	78.68	21.32	100%
	29.30	10.86	21.38	9.68	0.00	9.6	27.72	10.17	20.27
Others	50.28	49.72	100%	65.00	35.00	100%	51.07	48.93	100%
	50.14	65.92	56.91	41.93	38.89	40.82	49.48	64.21	55.74
Total	57.0	43.0	100%	63.0	37.0	100%	58.00	42.00	100%
	100%	100%	100%	100%	100%	100%	100%	100%	100%

respondents of both the sexes reside in urban area. In rural areas 47.38 women respondents are unaware of these schemes against 44.63% women in urban area.

Lack of proper communication with the scavengers is the main reason for their ignorance about these welfare programmes. The district level unit of Government should take the initiative in properly briefing scavengers about the programmes in operation for their upliftment. The office of Municipal Corporation/Nigam and their residential locality can be the appropriate place to impart information regarding welfare schemes to the scavengers. Such information could also be spread by voluntary organisations.

Table 9.3 shows the sources of information regarding Government Welfare Schemes. Only 27% respondents were aware of the schemes. 57% urban males were aware of the schemes against 63% males in the rural area. 8.20% respondents got the information from political workers. Almost all of them reside in urban area. N.G.Os' role in this work was marginal and only 1.49% respondents were benefited by it in the rural and urban area taken together. 4.32% respondents got the information from the government agencies out of which 62.06% reside in rural area. Electronic media has imparted information to 9.98% respondents and they all reside in urban area. Newspapers have been the source for information to 20.27% respondents out of which almost all reside in urban area. About 55.74% of the total respondents had the information through other sources like relatives and by other members in and outside their community.

Lack of information regarding different Government welfare schemes still persists in this community. Formal agencies which are responsible for awareness building are not efficient.

Table 9.4 shows the availability of different schemes. Education facility is available to 37.95% of the scavenger children in the age bracket of 6-14 years in the urban area and to 34.44% children in the rural area. 27.80% children in the urban area and 12.00% children in the rural area have been benefited from free books and food facility. Only 4.30% respondents in the urban area and 0.22% in the rural area were aware of the functioning of adult education centre.

Scavengers are not prepared to educate their children. They are

Table 9.4: Table Showing Availability of Schemes

Sl. No.	Category	Schemes								
		Education for Children below 14 Yrs.			Free Clothes, Books & Food Facility			Adult Education Centre		
		Yes	No	Total	Yes	No	Total	Yes	No	Total
		37.95	62.05	100%	27.40	72.60	100%	4.30	95.70	100%
1.	Urban	759	1241	2000	556	1452	2008	86	1914	2000
		83.04	80.79	81.7	91.15	78.57	81.7	98.85	81.00	81.7
		34.44	65.56	100%	12.00	88.00	100%	0.22	99.78	100%
2.	Rural	155	295	450	54	396	450	1	449	450
		16.96	19.21	18.3	8.85	21.43	18.3	1.15	19.00	18.3
		37.30	62.70	100%	25.00	75.00	100%	3.60	96.40	100%
	All	914	1536	2450	610	1840	2450	87	2363	2450
		100%	100%	100%	100%	100%	100%	100%	100%	100%

Table 9.5: Table Showing Benefit from Provision in Relation to Different Categories of Respondent

	Application of Modern Tools			Implementation of Minimum Wages			Professional Training			Loan Facility		
	Yes	No	Total	Yes	No	Total	Yes	No	Total	Yes	No	Total
	28.85	71.15	100%	41.00	59.00	100%	3.95	96.05	100%	1.30	98.70	100%
Urban	577	1423	2000	820	1100	2000	79	1921	2000	26	1974	2000
	98.46	76.34	81.7	87.61	77.94	81.70	100.00	81.02	81.79	6.30	81.47	81.7
	2.00	98.00	100%	25.78	74.22	100%	0.00	100.00	100%	0.22	99.78	100%
Rural	9	441	450	116	334	450	0	450	450	1	449	450
	1.54	23.66	18.3	12.39	22.06	18.3	0.00	18.98	18.3	3.70	18.53	18.3
	24.00	76.00	100%	38.21	61.79	100%	3.22	96.8	100%	1.10	98.9	100%
Total	586	1864	2450	936	1514	2450	79	2371	2450	27	2423	2450
	100%	100%	100%	100%	100%	100%	100%	100%	100%	100%	100%	100%

not aware of the value of education. Most of them live from day to day. They do not think of the future and do not strive for better living. It has been noticed that the parents restrict the education of girls to avoid a potentially uncomfortable situation in which the daughter develops an aversion for the traditional occupation of her caste. Despite all the budgetary provisions, distribution scheme of free books and food does not exist. This scheme was launched with the sole purpose of attracting children of the weaker communities towards education but it has proved to be a fiasco.

For those scavengers who are illiterate and old, education has no meaning. Their children also suffer due to prejudice. An attempt was made to reorient them towards education through the channel of adult education. The number of A.E.Cs. is small. Its impact is negligible.

Table 9.5 reveals the benefits from different welfare provisions accruing to the respondents belonging to different categories. About 28.86% respondents in the urban area were provided mechanical tools to work against 2% respondents in the rural area. In urban area 41.00% respondents were of the opinion that Minimum Wages Act has been implemented as against 25.78% respondents in the rural area. Only 3.95% respondents in the urban area received professional training. 1.30% and 0.22% respondents received loan in urban and rural area respectively.

It is mandatory for every Municipal Corporation/Nigam to provide mechanical tools to the scavengers for work as per the accepted recommendations of different commissions and committees, especially the Malkani Committee. In most of the Corporations/ Nigams these facilities are not available and the scavengers are left with the only option to operate manualy. For scavengers who are working privately in urban area and for those scavengers who are working in the rural area, implementation of minimum wages is a distant dream. It is only the bargaining ability of the scavengers which counts for getting the wages.

Under the provisions of the rehabilitation programme due emphasis has been given to the income generating schemes for the scavengers for which training and financial assistance are the two important features. The National Scheduled Castes and Scheduled Tribes Finance and Development Corporation (NSFDC) looks after both these aspects with the assistance of the local Welfare department. Despite the fact that without implementation of adequate training programme no occupational shift can be sought, the outcome is quite discouraging and confined to the urban areas. Likewise, those who are trained or otherwise interested in financial assistance, obtaining loan is not an easy task.

Table 9.6: Table Showing Benefits availed from different Government Schemes and Acts

Schemes	Response		
	Yes	No	Total
Distribution of Excess Land	37 8.22%	413 91.78%	450
Benefit of Bataidari Act	05 1.11%	445 98.88%	450
Benefit from Distribution of Animals	70 15.55%	380 84.44%	450
Financial Assistance to Start Cottage Industries	30 6.66%	420 93.33%	450

Table 9.6 shows the benefit accrued to the scavengers from different Government schemes in the rural area. About 8.22% respondents received land from the Government which was acquired under the Ceiling Act. Benefit of Bataidari Act was availed by only 1.11% respondents. 15.55% received animals from the Block under the I.R.D.P. Scheme. Financial assistance to start a cottage industry was provided to 6.66% respondents.

In comparison to other scheduled castes, very few scavengers got land from the Government for cultivation purpose. The reason may be their reluctance to take up agriculture work. Engagement of this community in agriculture is new and therefore, the number of beneficiaries availing the Bataidari Act benefit is small. Distribution of animals from the Block level is required to effect an occupational change in this community. There are different schemes for financial assistance to this community but due to multiple reasons, both in Government and the scavengers, the result is discouraging.

Table 9.7: Table showing whether anyone from the household is receiving Old Age Pension

Category	Response		
	Yes	No	All
Urban	85	1915	2000
	18.06%	81.94%	
Rural	28	422	450
	24.78%	75.22%	
Total	113	2337	2450
	4.61%	95.39%	

Table 9.7 reveals the number of persons receiving old-age pension. About 4.61% respondents are receiving old-age pension. Among them 18.06% reside in the urban area and the rest in the rural area.

This pension scheme is for all people above 60 years who are below the poverty line. During the study it was found that most of the scavengers families were still not aware about old-age pension scheme. Some of them even reported that despite their repeated efforts the concerned officials were not approving their name. In most of the cases, for getting the name approved one has to grease the palm of government functionaries. Payment of pension is not regular and on most of the occasions the pensioner receives it after three to six months. For those scavengers who are eligible, this is the only means for their survival. Due to irregular payment of pension they have to face great hardship.

Summing Up

While there is no denying the fact that some significant work has been done in the post-Independent India to liberate scavengers from the social bondage, the problem persists as a continuing disgrace for the nation. Many welfare schemes launched for the liberation of scavengers have not made any significant dent on the problem.

With the commencement of the Gandhi Centenary Year in 1969 emphasis was laid on the emancipation of the scavengers. Another effort was made by the Government of India in 1968 by promoting a special campaign for conversion of dry latrines into water flush ones with the objective of relieving the scavengers. Apart from this, the training and financial assistance scheme under the rehabilitation programme also gave impetus for the overall development of this community.

It has been found that the attitude of the scavengers themselves has been a strong deterrent to their liberation and rehabilitation primarily due to the following reasons:

1. Since head-loading has been a way of life for the scavengers, they fear that their livelihood may be affected if they try to change their occupation.
2. The scavengers have a fatalistic outlook due to lack of education and proper guidance regarding the openings for alternate employment. On account of this they resist any change.
3. Vast majority of the scavengers are unaware of various measures undertaken by the Government in respect of financial assistance, training and reservation in employment.

10

ROLE OF NON-GOVERNMENT ORGANISATION'S (NGO's)

Background and Significance of NGOs

The phenomenon of non-government organisation (NGOs), variously structured, named and categorised, is not new either in India or outside. In India the struggle for national independence was accompanied by many movements for social, educational and cultural reform, sometimes challenging and sometimes building on earlier tradition. Movements led by Gandhi, Ambedkar and others effectively combined programmes for social reform with wider movements of social and political mobilisation. These traditions have continued to provide inspiration to later generations in India.

The past two decades have witnessed a rapid expansion in the number of NGOs as well as in the range of programmes and issues which they take up. There has been major growth of interest in their potential capacity to assist in development programmes of Government and international agencies and among intellectuals, professionals, social activists and others concerned with overcoming poverty and injustice.

Voluntarism in the 1990s is therefore, marked by new demands and responsibilities as it is by opportunities. What started as social reform has veered towards development and mobilization. New directions such as the constitutional amendments for Panchayati Raj will be impossible to implement without the capacitation by NGOs at the grass-roots. Devolving decision-making processes closer to communities has in some countries put the voluntary sector at the centre of development (neighbouring Bangladesh is an example) and of the political process. While the situation in India may appear less dramatic, change is unmistakeable. Influential donors see NGOs as an often more effective alternative for channelling their assistance, particularly after the candid admission by the late Rajiv Gandhi that less than 20% of India's disbursements through Government-controlled anti-poverty programmes actually reach the intended beneficiaries.

What this means is that the sector can today attract support for its ideas and experiments without quite the same barriers of resistance as yesterday. This is particularly useful as activities branch out into areas still unfamiliar such as gender and child rights environment, occupational and reproductive health, and consumer protection. Each new challenge brings greater opportunity demonstrated by the science education movements initiated by Kerala Sahitya Parishad in the South and Eklavya in Madhya Pradesh, the environmental awareness activities of the Centre of Environmental Education in Gujarat, and INTACH's work with planning authorities in several centres of historic and ecological importance. Available technologies, from computer networks to indigenous knowledge that has been long neglected, are being applied in experiments much as those towards sustainable livelihoods by Development Alternatives, or to foster innovator-entrepreneur linkage through the Grass-roots Innovations Augmentation Network (GIAN) at the Indian Institute of Management, Ahmedabad. Support institutions for new skills and technologies have become available through management institutes, colleges of engineering and design, and research bodies including the Indian Space Research Organisation (ISRO). New financial mechanisms are being devised, specially tailored to the abilities of NGOs such as women's banks established by SEWA in Ahmedabad and a variety of micro credit schemes, many inspired by Bangladesh model. In the search for alternatives relevant to a new millennium, Mahatma Gandhi's words find repeated utterance: "The earth has enough for everyone's need, but not enough for anyone's greed". The expansion of a development agenda has acquired fresh and powerful relevance ever since world leaders put their signatures to Agenda 21 at RIO in 1992. If alternatives are urgent for survival of dignity of millions on this planet, India's voluntary sector can turn its strengths to much more than demonstrating efficiency in a mainstream defined by market forces. The mainstream itself can be encouraged to change from being greed-based to need-based. India can help establish that development derives sustainability from people mobilised on their own terms and put in charge of their own destiny. That is the tryst long awaited by so many here and in every part of the world.

In India some voluntary agencies have taken up activities bearing on the well-being of scavengers. Unfortunately, their number is not large enough to meet the challenges posed by the position of scavengers in Indian society, their life and working conditions. The functioning of some such agencies in Bihar is detailed below.

Sulabh International Social Service Organisation

The Sulabh International Social Service Organisation is the largest nationally and internationally recognised pan-India social service outfit with 35,000 volunteers on the rolls who work to promote human rights, environmental sanitation through education, training and awareness campaign. It has developed a scavenging-free two pits pourflush toilet (Sulabh Shauchalaya), safe and hygienic on site human waste disposal technology, a new concept of maintenance and construction of pay and use public toilets, popularly known as Sulabh Complex. It has set up an English-medium Public School in New Delhi to educate boys and girls from Valmiki families. The education provided is of high quality. The children mix with other children in the school. Thus, their isolation is reduced and they grow up as members of an integrated society.

The Sulabh technology has liberated so far 37,500 scavengers from the demeaning practice of physically cleaning and carrying human excreta. Sulabh has set up more than 3,100 pay and use community toilet complexes and about 8,00,000 Shauchalayas in private houses which are being used by more than ten million people every day. This novel self-sustaining system has also helped in ending the uncivilised practice of open-air defecation and keeping the urban life clean and livable, creating enormous impact on the environment and life of the people, specially those living in squatter colonies, the houseless and the people on the move or those at places of congregation.

The point 11 in the Government of India's 20-point Programme of 1986 relates to "Justice to Scheduled Castes and Scheduled Tribes". It is aimed at eradication of scavenging and undertaking special programmes for the rehabilitation of scavengers. Sulabh is fully involved in achieving this objective. Till now, Sulabh International has made 33 towns scavenging-free.

Its training organisation takes up liberation of scavengers by conversion of dry/bucket privies into Sulabh Shauchalayas and training and rehabilitation of liberated scavengers and their wards. Sulabh organises programmes to train them in various vocations such as driving, mechanic, tailoring, typing, computer, cane work, carpentry, leather work, mason etc. They are also educated in health, sanitation and personal hygiene. Sulabh established training institutes exclusively for scavengers at Patna and Mahavir Enclave, New Delhi.

The liberation of scavengers and their rehabilitation in other professions is not enough. Not less important is the upgradation of their social status so that they can be absorbed into the mainstream of the society. Towards that end, Sulabh has persuaded a large number of eminent persons including judges, politicians, ministers, journalists and social workers to "socially adopt" one scavenger family each and help them to get jobs and other benefits permissible under the law. The adopter visits the adopted (and *vice versa*) openly so that they can get social respectability. This programme is getting a very encouraging response.

The Sulabh Shauchalaya movement was started in Bihar by Dr. Bindeshwar Pathak who was deeply inspired by Mahatma Gandhi's idea of Bhangi Mukti. In the early 1970s, he developed the requisite technology for setting up pourflush toilets. The work was initiated in September 1973 in the Ara Municipality. The Bihar Government was impressed by the results and funds were allotted to local bodies for the conversion of service latrines. In 1974 the Government of Bihar recognised the Sulabh Shauchalaya Sansthan as the catalytic agency for this work. During 1974 to 1988, 1.86 lakh dry latrines were converted thereby liberating 3,000 scavengers in 15 towns of Bihar. In fact, the non-availability of funds has been the main constraint otherwise all the four lakh dry latrines could have been converted in the entire state.

Details of Work Completed by Sulabh International Social Service Organisation in Bihar (up to March, 1998)

1.	Scavengers liberated	4,500
2.	Number of Sulabh Social Workers	3,000
3.	Human excreta-based biogas plants	5
4.	Towns made scavenger-free	26
5.	Districts where Sulabh works	All districts of the State
6.	Total number of Sulabh Shauchalayas	2,03,622
7.	Number of Towns with only Sulabh Shauchalaya Complexes	116
8.	Number of Complexes being operated and maintained by Sulabh	249

The work of the Sulabh International has largely been confined to urban areas. However, the organisation has constructed 1,198 toilets in the primary and middle schools of Bihar at the behest of the State Education Department.

For the rural areas Sulabh organised a training programme for village masons so that they could construct toilets based on Sulabh technology in the villages.

Ambedkar Institute of Research and Rehabilitation, Yarpur, Patna

Ambedkar Institute of Research and Rehabilitation was established in 1982-83. Dr. C.K. Jha and Smt. Geeta Shrivastava are the Chairman and Secretary of the Institute. The main objectives of this organisation is training in tailoring and typing for Balmikis and others. Bihar Scheduled Castes Development Corporation, Patna sponsored training in typing and tailoring for 40 persons in 1987. The duration of training for typing and shorthand is six months while for tailoring it is one year.

T.M. Samajik Seva Sansthan, Motihari

Tirthankar Mahavir Samajik Seva Sansthan is headed by Dr. M.M.P. Shrivastava, a former Director of Agriculture. This organisation is a registered NGO. Its main objective is promotion of sanitation, construction of public toilets, urinals and drains and removal of the practice of manual scavenging, liberation of scavengers and their rehabilitation. It is also interested in a large number of activities in the field of rural development with particular reference to the weaker section of the population. It also undertakes programmes for the creation of awareness about septic latrines. Its area of operation is spread over a number of villages in three blocks of the East Champaran district. In each village a number of families have been identified. These are from the most deprived sections of the community. Members of this organisation take special care to involve the community in all development work. Their particular focus is on women who are being trained to become catalyst in sanitation programmes. Liberated scavengers are being given training in various cottage industries such as tailoring, leather work, shorthand and typing and making of agarbati, leaf plates and candles. These activities have been taken up under the TRYSEM Scheme. They are making special efforts to change the attitude of the scavengers and to give them hope for a better future.

Ambedkar Suraksha Manch, West Boring Canal Road, Patna

Ambedkar Suraksha Manch is located in Patna. Shri Jodhraj Valmiki is the Chairman and Shri Girija Shankar Prasad is the Secretary of this Manch. The main objective of the organisation is to protect the constitutional rights of the *Mahadalits*, to prevent them from exploitation, atrocities and injustice and speed up socio-economic and educational development of the scavengers, streamline the Mahadalits in national integration and creating harmonious relationship. Irrespective of caste, creed and religion all who belong to below poverty line are Mahadalits and the main duty of the organisation is to serve them.

For the all-round development of Mahadalits the Manch organised one-day fast on 14th July 1998. The main demands of the organisation were :

1. Regular payment of salary of scavengers working in Corporation, Municipalities and Notified Area Committees and quick implementation of all the facilities like Government servants.
2. To abolish manual scavenging (head-loading) system and rehabilitate those scavengers.
3. To constitute State-level Safai Karamchari Ayog as at the national level.
4. To abolish the reservation for the seats of Lok Sabha and Vidhan Sabha for those SC members and their dependants who have already enjoyed this facility for ten years.

Bihar Harijan Sevak Sangh (BHSS)

Bihar Harijan Sevak Sangh was founded in 1934. Mr. Jagdish Prasad Mahto is the Chairman of this organisation. The main objective of this organisation is integrated development of Harijan community. It has done a wonderful job in eradicating untouchability and entry of Harijans in the temples.

Bihar Harijan Sevak Sangh made a serious effort for the improvement of the status of scavengers. For this purpose it pressurised Government for providing wheel-barrows and other materials.

At present the Sangh is operating creches in Bihar. This scheme is for the scavenger community only. There is an arrangement of keeping 25 children in a creche. Whenever scavenger women go to attend their duty they keep their children in creche. After their duty hour they take back their children. Three creches have been working in Patna as mentioned below:

1. Ambedkar Colony, Patna City.

2. Raja Bazar, Shekhpura.
3. Punpun.

Mahila Vikas Samiti (MVS) (A Self-Help Group of Women Scavengers)

Mahila Vikas Samiti was set up with the help of the district administration as a voluntary agency of scavenger women in 1996. Smt. Gangiya Devi and Smt. Radha Devi are the Chairperson and Secretary. The membership fee is Rs. 20 per month. The Government of Bihar and the Bank of India, Mithapur assured financial assistance of Rs. 20,000 to MVS to open its account. With the efforts of MVS orders have been passed for the construction of 236 houses under Indira Awas Yojana. The organisation imparted training to 30 women in tailoring and stitching. The Family Planning Association of India provided one sewing machine to this agency. Rs. 300 each was given to 20 women for starting some business. However, the amount was too small and it was misspent. Due to lack of money training work is closed now.

The MVS organises health camp and helps needy persons occasionally. There is a non-formal education centre run by this organisation. There are two teachers who are paid Rs. 300 per month. 'CENCORED' Patna provides books for non-formal education.

11
CASE STUDIES

Community Case Studies

1. *Rajasthani Scavengers of Ranchi*

Population

The approximate number of households of Rajasthani scavengers is 190 living in different localities of Ranchi.

Table 11.1: Showing Number of Households in Different Locations of Ranchi

Location	No. of Households
Balmiki Nagar (Harmoo Road)	90
Bariyatu Housing Colony	25
Medical Colony	15
Harmoo Housing Colony	30
Ranchi Town (Scattered)	30
Total	190

Living and Working Conditions

Rajasthani scavengers have been living in a good environment compared to other scavengers. Their houses and surroundings were clean. Family members of the scavengers were neat and clean. Scavengers pay Rs. 200 as house rent but there are no facilities.

Many houses have not been repaired for the past 50-60 years. They got this housing facility on rent from the Corporation. The working conditions of scavengers are not good. Municipal Corporation does not provide boots, gloves and other necessary equipment for cleaning work. All the scavengers have to work 8 hours. The working hour is 6-11 a.m. and 2-5 p.m. There is no weekly holiday for daily wage scavengers, although they have been working from approximately 15-20 years. Vacancies exist but they are working as daily labourers.

Scavengers were unhappy with the working conditions and benefits given by the Municipal Corporation. They are being paid 75% of their pay at the time of pension. No D.A. is included in the pension. This is why only Rs. 140 is paid to the class 3rd and 4th grade employees. So far as payment of pension is concerned, it is paid after 2-3 years of retirement. In some cases payment is not made even after 2-3 years unless scavengers file court case against the Corporation. They do not get dress, gumboot and soap. The official staff suppress the scavengers. As far as holidays are concerned, clerks and official staff avail these facilities while scavengers do not get them. They have to work at the time of festivals also and no overtime or leave adjustment is done by the office staff. Provident Fund of the staff is also not deposited even if there are funds available in the Corporation.

Although there is ban on alcoholism among Marwari scavengers, they take liquor in the evening. Very few people take alcohol during day time. They argue they take liquor to get some relief from fatigue.

Migration

Marwari scavengers migrated approximately 60-70 years back from Rajasthan. The business class people left that place for business so scavengers became out of job. Some of the businessmen of Marwar came to Ranchi. Owing to unemployment in Rajasthan, the scavengers came to Ranchi. Due to illiteracy people started their own occupation like scavenging. They were having neither skill nor education for other jobs. At that very time the Eastern Command shifted to Ranchi and these people were employed there as scavengers. Many people started working in factories, hospitals and other places.

Head-Loading

Although head-loading exists in Ranchi town, Rajasthani scavengers do not work as head-loaders. This was disclosed by the scavengers at the time of case study.

Impact of Welfare Measures

Old-age pension is given to some of the members of scavenger community. Scholarship is also provided to the students of scavengers who go to government schools. But no coaching or training has been given to the Marwari scavengers. About 100 youths are matriculate. They have been looking for job in different offices but have not succeeded. Ten persons of this community received government loan for tempo and one for S.T.D. unit. So far as efforts of NGOs are concerned, *Sulabh International Social Service Organisation* has constructed *Sulabh Shauchalayas* in their hamlets. They complained that they are being deprived from the facilities or provisions meant for the welfare of scavengers community. They cited an example of a public distribution shop which had been allotted to a higher caste person in preference to scavengers.

Main Problems

Umeployment among the youth is the main problem faced by the scavengers. Illiteracy is prevalent in the scavenger society. Due to illiteracy scavengers are being exploited at the time of payment of salary in the offices of the Municipal Corporation.

Suggestions

Scavengers should be educated through 'Ratri Pathshala' (Night

School) so that exploitation by the officials of the Corporation might be reduced. The scavengers do not get the amount written in the register. They are exploited by the Cashier, Sanitary Inspector and other official staff of the Municipal Corporation. Scavengers cannot oppose them. If they oppose the Sanitary Inspector, he will not give work to them or they will be marked absent from duty.

Moreover, Head Clerk, Cashier and Sanitary Inspector are the money-lenders and they recover the loan at the time of salary payment. It would have been better if their salary would have been paid through the bank.

Some welfare schemes should be started through the Corporation. Training is the need of the scavenger youth.

Organisation of the Marwari Scavengers

Marwari scavengers have formed Harijan Balmiki Samaj in Ranchi. Through this organisation they provide bedding, utensils and other necessary things at the time of marriage ceremony in the house of any member of the Balmiki Samaj.

Rajasthani scavengers pay much attention to worship. Whenever they return from their duty they do not enter their house without taking bath.

2. *Muslim Scavengers of Biharsharif*

Biharsharif is the district headquarters of Nalanda. Originally its name was Vihar or Bihar and the word 'Sharif' had been added to its name by the Muslims as a number of shrines and durgahs are located in and around this town.

Along with Asharafs and Atrafs or Ajlafs, a considerable number of Arzals reside in this town. Among Muslims the Ashraf category consists of the lineages of Saiyeds, Sheikhs, Pathans, Maliks and Mirzas, all of which claim foreign origin. The Atraf or Ajlaf category consists of the indigenous clean occupational groups converted to Islam and includes the so-called backward class Muslims. The converted untouchables were given the name of Arzal and even after embracing Islam there was little change in their social standing and ranking. The scavengers are also included in Arzal category and in the Muslim community they are generally called *Mehtar* or *Halalkhor*. These Muslim scavengers may consist of either local Bhangis converted to Islam or those Mehtar or Halalkhor who migrated from other places to this town in the hope of better earning.

Some Muslim scavengers reported that they have migrated from their native villages. The main reason for migration was lack of employment in the village. Having come to Biharsharif Halalkhor women started working as scavengers in the Municipality. Halalkhors live mainly in the hamlets of Saluganj, Katraper, Soh, Pahariper and Nanuatoli. The estimated number of households is 164.

Table 11.2: Showing Mohallawise Households

Mohallas	Number of Households
Bagnabad	40
Soh	12
Pahariper	6
Nanuatoli	6
Choti Saluganj and	
Saluganj Kharihani	50
Domkhana (Gulshan Bag, Katra)	48
Kagaji Mohalla	2
Total	164

A rough estimate suggests that the total population of Muslim scavengers is around 1,100.

Living and Working Conditions

No male Halalkhor works in the municipality. Male members are engaged in other professions like toy making, mason, private work, painting, motor mechanic etc. Bidi industry is important in

Biharsharif. Both men and women do this work with their children.

Majority of the women scavengers in this community have been living in rented houses. Some scavengers have their own houses but due to non-payment of salary by the municipality they had to mortgage their paternal houses and now they live on rent in the same house.

In the Katra Mohalla 48 scavengers live in rooms given by the municipality but the condition of rooms is not good. Most rooms have no tiles. During rainy season most of the rooms were full of water due to leakage of the roof. Although the municipality installed a toilet of 6 seats for the scavengers, its condition is also very bad. There was no roof on the toilet, no arrangement of water and electricity for the scavengers.

Most Muslim scavengers are illiterate. Some of them are semi-illiterate, as they can recite *Quran* and put their signature with difficulty. It is significant to point out here that in the traditional Muslim society the members of this occupational group were permitted to read or recite *Quran* provided they took bath and removed the pollution or Nejasat from their clothes and bodies. This practice is found at other places also. In Uttar Pradesh, for example, "Muslim Bhangis are allowed to learn the Quran, but they are not expected to teach it" (Ansari, 1960: 50). This usage motivated a few of these female scavengers to read Quran, if not the whole text, a part of it. But after their liberation from this activity a marked change is found in respect of literacy.

There is no arrangement of education for the scavenger children. There is no government school nearby the *Mohalla*. They are unable to arrange paper, pen and books due to poverty. Scavengers are not getting their salary from the municipality for the past 16 months. The duration of work is 8 hours for them.

Although service latrine is available in some of the houses in Biharsharif but Muslim scavengers do not clean service latrines. The way of living of Muslim women scavengers is similar to that of other Muslim women. The culture is more or less same. As they are working women they do not observe purdah as other women do.

They have been living in a dirty and congested place. Majority of the scavengers have been living in rented rooms. 8 to 10 persons live in one room or two rooms. They cook their food in the same room. Some houses were kachcha and some pucca. Their toilets were mostly dirty. There was no arrangement of light and safe drinking water. Although they are sanitation workers, their own hamlets do not have any sanitation. When they come after performing the scavenging work, people do not allow them to take bath on the community water tap.

Muslim scavengers have interest in their children's education but due to lack of food and clothes they are unable to educate them.

Relationship with Hindu Scavengers

The scavengers and their family members were treated as untouchables in the Muslim community and by caste Hindus. They were not allowed to sit or mix with the clean castes or occupational groups. Except the job site, they did not have social interaction with their Hindu counterparts. Neither do they invite them on the occasion of marriage, aquiaa or circumcision, nor they were invited on such occasions by Hindu Bhangis. Moreover, on occasions like funeral or Shradh ceremonies also there was no such interaction. After liberation, they feel that they are no more regarded as untouchable Muslims. They go to the places of religious congregations and offer prayers in the mosque or durgah. But the caste Hindus still do not have any social interaction with them. As there is no untouchability in the Muslim community, they attend the festivals with other higher Muslim castes. They celebrate Id and other festivals with them.

Government Welfare Programmes

Muslim scavengers complained that they are not being provided those facilities which were availed by Hindu scavengers. They cited an example of Scheduled Caste Development Finançe Corporation (AJAVINI) which provides training and loan facilities to Hindu scavengers but Halalkhor scavengers are deprived of any benefit as they are not scheduled caste, although they are doing the same work which Hindu scavengers do.

Problems

1. The municipality has not paid the salary of Muslim scavengers for the past 14-15 months.
2. There is no housing for the bulk of scavengers. They are unable to pay their house-rent.
3. Muslim scavengers complained that retired personnel do not get the entry of their wards in the municipality. Other persons are appointed in their place.
4. Women scavengers do not have the service book. This is why they do not know how much money is deducted and how much money is deposited in which item. They have no proof of the deduction. Officers of the municipality do not pay attention to their grievances.

No arrear and bonus is paid to the scavengers. The municipality provides dress once in five years. Corruption is alleged to be rampant in the municipality. While clerks and other officials of the municipality take their salary the scavengers do not get their salary. Even equipments for the work is not supplied properly by the officials. Office provides basket (*daliya*) once in six months while spade and broom are given only after two years. Officials of the municipality always insist on the purchase of broom at their own cost otherwise attendance will be cut. Owing to irregular payment of salary the Muslim scavengers have to take loan at high rate of interest *i.e.* 25% per month, when their children are ill and sometimes for their maintenance, they have to mortagage their goods. This situation always arises in the family of scavengers.

Muslim scavengers of Biharsharif were of the opinion that loan for self-employment should be arranged so that they can start some business of their own, other than providing education to their children. Lack of proper education among the scavengers is the main reason for their mass exploitation.

Perception of Change

3. *Old and Experienced Leaders*

Shri Jodhraj Valmiki in his mid-sixties is a celebrated figure in the scavenger community. He was only seven years old when his parents migrated to Bihar from Rajasthan in search of employment. Since then his family is settled at Patna. He belongs to Pawar clan and has married in the family of a Marwari scavenger of Hazaribagh. Out of his five children, four are married in the families with similar antecedents. His eldest son is working at a creche in Patna city which is financed by the Ministry of Welfare. The second son is working at the Bank of Baroda, while the third is engaged in a petty business in Rajasthan and the fourth is a student of B.A. His only daughter is married at Ranchi in a Rajasthani scavenger family. At present, he holds positions in several non-governmental organisations including Ambedkar Institute of Research and Rehabilitation, Patna and Safai Majdoor Sangh, Patna. He is the founder President of Naya Bharat Party, a political outfit for the political empowerment of the scavengers.

After completing his middle school education he joined Patna Municipal Corporation as a *Safai Karamchari* in 1953.There he was face to face with the plight of scavenger community, which was hitherto unknown to him. At the same time besides untouchability the economic backwardness of the community was a great constraint. The bulk of scavengers used to take debt from the money-lenders who were from the Yadav caste. For repayment of debt and the interest on it, the scavengers had to sacrifice their entire salary. The local administration and the police was ineffective in curbing the money-lenders' activities. Shri Valmiki took up this issue with the help of some other like-minded scavengers. Initially, they forced the money-lenders not to enter the campus of the Municipal Corporation and it was followed by the refusal of debt interest payment. With the support of Harijan Sevak Sangh every member of the scavenger community whole-heartedly supported this crusade and for some time the money-lenders were removed from the scene. This situation could not sustained and the money-lenders reappeared.

He has struggled since 1957 for his community when he first joined Safai Majdoor Sangh as Secretary for Patna sub-division. In 1962, he joined Hind Sweeper Sevak Samaj and later in 1965 he joined Harijan Sevak Sangh as teacher-cum-writer. While working in Harijan Sevak Sangh he formed Harijan Sahyog Sangh as its wing. Shri Valmiki joined Harijan Sevak Sangh on the invitation of Shri N.R. Malkani who during his visit to Patna in 1965 was very much impressed by his work.

After leaving Harijan Sevak Sangh in 1968, Shri Valmiki started selling ready-made garments at Patna on footpath. He used to bring these from Calcutta. Occasionally he used to visit the nearby rural area for selling garments. Later he changed his occupation and joined Apna Bazar as a sweeper. After that, he joined the Post and Telegraph Department in 1969 on the post of sewerman. Here he joined the labour union and worked for it till 1995. In between, he was also member of the evaluation team meant for the evaluation of Special Component Plan for the scavengers till 1990. Since 1995, he is associated with Sulabh International. He has been nominated as a member of the People's Commission on Abolition of Scavenging.

Under his able guidance Ambedkar Suraksha Manch was formed in 1995 and he was elected its first President. The main objective of the Manch is to protect the constitutional rights of the Mahadalits, to stop their exploitation, atrocities and injustice and speed up socio-economic and educational development of scavengers, to streamline the Mahadalits in national integration and create harmonious relationship. Irrespective of caste, creed and religion all who belong to below poverty line are Mahadalits and the main duty is to serve them.

Another major issue at that time was the addiction to alcohol. Shri Valmiki organised a group of people who used to go from one locality to another under his leadership and make people aware about the ill-effects of alcohol. Later some women also joined this movement. The scavengers were asked to take oath that they will not drink alcohol any more, and thus drinking became a punishable offence in their community. Community meetings were regularly organised at night. This campaign by Shri Valmiki made the liquor traders worried and they started putting pressure on him, but in vain. The movement lost its momentum and the scavenger community returned to the alcohol culture. At present many of the scavenger families are earning their livelihood by selling alcohol illegally. For the crusader like Shri Valmiki this situation is painful.

During his tenure at Harijan Sevak Sangh where he stayed from 1965 to 1968, he conducted an experiment for removing untouchability, one of the burning issues of that time. He collected some scavengers and it was planned that every day they will visit one tea-shop to take tea. Serving tea in glass tumbler to untouchables was not in vogue at that time. They were served tea in earthen pots and were not permitted to enter the shops. As per the plan, the scavengers started visiting the tea-shops, requesting the owner to allow them to sit on the benches and serve them tea in the glass tumblers. In the beginning, some tea-shop owners were reluctant to serve but when they were informed about the law against the prohibition of untouchability, the shop owners relented. One shop owner knew that Valmikis do not accept eatables from the Dhobi. He brought one Dhobi to serve tea to the untounchables to counter the efforts of the Valmikis to overcome the stigma of untouchability. Shri Valmiki countered this move by accepting tea from the hands of the Dhobi. Thus, the effort of the tea-shop owner to oppose the Bhangi move was frustrated. Each day one new shop was visited and this chain continued till one Marwari tea-shop owner totally refused to do so. Scavengers continued their pressure for three days but the owner was not ready to serve them tea as to others. Then a local Congress leader was asked to intervene. Due to his effort the Marwari tea-shop owner agreed to the demand. Later it was found that all the glass tumblers were broken after the use. Shri Valmiki feels that the symbolic protest was a success and definitely it boosted the scavengers psychologically. Thus, one small effort by Shri Valmiki changed the mind-set of the Valmikis and other higher castes.

About the future of his Naya Bharat Party, Shri Valmiki is not very optimistic. His own personal experience about untouchability is still fresh in his memory. He gives the example of the tea episode by concluding that the society which failed to give him tea in a glass tumbler cannot accept him as their leader or representative. Another dimension of the problem is that other scheduled caste people also do not wish to identify themselves with scavengers. The Paswan are the socially, economically and politically dominant group among the scheduled castes in Bihar. According to Shri Valmiki the Paswan leaders do not want to assist the scavengers in their upliftment process. Apart from these flaws, Shri Valmiki feels that the participation of scavengers in voting process has increased substantially, especially in urban areas.

Much is being made for the upliftment of the scavengers but Shri Valmiki feels that it is not enough. Similar to other caste, Hindus education is a major issue for the scavengers. He himself is striving in this field since 1969 through NGOs. The magazine "Mukti Sandesh" edited by him is laudable effort in this direction. He feels that on the issue of liberation, government has failed to tackle it properly and the desired target has not been achieved. The State Government is not utilising the funds properly and it would have been better if the government might have asked the NGOs like Sulabh International to take up the training and rehabilitation programme. Shri Valmiki feels that *Sampurn Kranti* is the only way out for the scavengers and for this they will have to organise.

4. Shri Jagdish Hari is one among the almost 2,000 strong scavenger community residing in the Bhagalpur town. An old man in his early seventies, he has vast knowledge about his community besides the functioning of Municipal Corporation where he worked for 40 years, way back from 1948 when he joined it till 1988, the year of his retirement. He regards himself fortunate as he was elevated to the post of Chief Sanitary Inspector from which post he retired. For almost five decades he was associated with Harijan Sevak Sangh and many other like-minded organisations working for the betterment of the scavenger community. He also authored many articles and participated in many seminars at different places. An effective orator, his deep knowledge of welfare ethic keeps him in demand. His association with Prof. Malkani during his visit to

Bhagalpur is ever fresh in his memory which he never fails to recall.

His perception of change in the scavenger community is given below:

"Before independence, the scavengers were thought to be a group which was assigned a particular task in which it had a monopoly. During British days they were a functional caste and they were remunerated as such. But after independence, contrary to the hue and cry for this underprivileged community nothing substantial was done. Gandhiji took up their cause and after his death, for almost two decades the Harijan Sevak Sangh honestly tried to fulfil his dream, but later on the indifferent approach of different governments towards this community watered down the whole effort. Despite the fact that many committees were constituted under the able chairmanship of eminent personalities, nothing substantial was implemented. The working condition in the 1960s and 1970s was quite inhuman. Both males and females used to carry drum, tin and *tasla* full of human excreta on their head and had to walk for almost 2-3 km for its disposal. Throughout this exercise the head-loader has to face ostracism of the society for which they used to work. But after the implementation of the Malkani Commission report, mechanical tools made the exercise easier. Yet head-loading did not stop. In government offices, the scavenger was not allowed to enter the chamber of the officials in their presence. After the work, they were asked to sit on the outskirts of the premises. Even talking to them was considered polluting. The locality where they lived was rarely visited by the people of other communities since it was in poor shape. But no efforts were made to clean these localities, it was thought that the basic requirements like drinking water, electricity, school etc., are not required for these people and, therefore, it was seldom cared for by the local authorities. *Ganda Hai, Ganda Hi Kam Karega* was the view of other people".

Many changes have taken place in different day-to-day affairs of the scavengers. Like other communities the scavengers had their own perception regarding these changes.

In the present decade, an effort has been made by the State

government to make education accessible to this community. It is an effective measure for the upliftment of this community. Many have also shown positive response, but on the whole the scavengers have another argument "*Padha Likha To Bojh Hai, Ganda Kam Bhi Nahi Karta*". They cite many examples of youths who after completing high school or getting a degree are without jobs. Their education is preventing them from continuing the unclean occupation, further making them a burden on the family. Such experiences hamper the spread of education in the scavenger community. They have a long way to go for establishing the credibility of education by evolving a mechanism to absorb the educated in suitable jobs.

In contrast to the general assumption that the scavengers are not eager to avail the welfare schemes, the ground level reality is the opposite. Apart from "Garima Yojana" no other scheme yielded the desired results. The local level officials failed to encourage the scavengers to avail the facility. The official publicity medium failed to attract the target groups. Very few, who were working in government sector, got the opportunity to avail the benefit. Thus, rehabilitation programmes for the scavengers need to cover all sections of the community. The need is to promote initiative and provide incentives to the scavengers for seeking training and self-employment with the assistance of the government and non-government agencies.

Through some constitutional changes, the Central Government has made certain provisions for political safeguards for this community which is a welcome step. Sense of political participation has also increased recently, but still the scavengers as such lack leadership. In the politics of scheduled castes, they are considered untouchables as far as decision-making and sharing of political power is concerned. Their poor economic condition and unwillingness to contribute physically in the political affairs further distances them from the political power. Similarly, in the trade union activities, despite the fact that they regard it feasible, they seldom prove to be able leaders and good followers. Mostly leaders from other communities champion the scavengers' cause thus depriving them from assimilating political culture. Attitudinal change and knowledge about political developments is foremost requirement in which the electronic and print media can play a major and decisive role. They are no more aloof from these media. People of older generation can also take initiative to bring about political understanding by telling them about their constitutional right.

Some effort was made to improve the working conditions under different schemes but at the district level, plans were not implemented properly. Apart from purchase of some mechanical tools the whole set-up remained unchanged. Payment of salaries on time is a distant dream and arrears are increasing day to day. After 1991, the State Government has stopped contributing its share and the Corporation is left with no other option but to generate funds from its own revenue. In the case of Bhagalpur, in the year 1972 there were 640 scavengers working with the Municipality but its strength shrank to 400 in the year 1998. This policy on the part of government not to employ the scavengers according to the requirement leads to unemployment. To drag out the youths from this vicious circle of unemployent, some alternative arrangements have to be made. Conversion of latrines was encouraged on a mass scale with a view to end the system of head-loading. But at the same time no proper scheme was made to rehabilitate the head-loaders. This has caused mass unemployment. The condition of the scavengers has deteriorated to a large extent due to unemployment. This condition is more painful than that of head-loading. *Bhukha Rakh Kar, Privartan Ki Baat Karte Hai* is the perception of the change process in this community. It makes them rebel against the government and society.

Social intercourse between the scavengers and other scheduled caste communities as well as others like Muslims has increased. They participate in each other's festivals, marriage and other ceremonies. There is no feeling of untouchability among them. A greater degree of inter-caste relations is noticed among the youths. They mingle with each other including inter-dining at restaurants. The impact of modernisation is evident in their dress and life-style. But for the scavengers the stigma of pollution sticks to them. Such stigma has been eroded in the urban set-up, but in rural areas it is still there.

The future of this community depends on the attitudinal change in the larger society. The entire society has to accept that the scavengers are a deprived section of the society and it is the duty of the whole system to make them stand on their own. Especially, this responsibility should be shared by the intellectuals to wipe out the age-old stigma attached with this community. Role of youths is equally important for upliftment of this community. They will have to come forward to break the age-old barriers.

5. *Rural Woman Elite*

Smt. Saugatiya Devi is resident of Chand Sarai village in the Mahua Block in the district of Vaishali. The village has a small population of nine odd scavenger families. It is merely due to the increase of the population that their dwellings look like a part of the village, rather the outskirt of the village which is dominated by upper castes. In her early fifties, she is no more engaged in scavenging, as her health does not permit it. A widow with three sons and three daughters-in-law along with half a dozen grandsons and granddaughters, she has vivid reminiscences about her community and neighbourhood. Some of the changes perceived by her are noted below.

Women in the rural areas are a much deprived lot especially among the scavengers. Women do not figure in the decision-making process. Her only advantage in the scavenger community is her ability to earn. This makes her important and thus she develops the power to resist in the male-dominated community. Apart from the earning ability the social approval to remarry according to her choice is also a vital factor to enhance her importance. On the whole, the position of women in the scavenger community is not uniform and does vary from family to family according to economic status. The position also varies in families of scavengers who are working outside. A sea-change can be witnessed in their family as almost all major decisions are taken by the better-half. These neo-migrated families put much emphasis on the girls' socialisation and it is hoped that in a generation or so the position of women among the scavengers will rise.

Scavenging as a profession has lost its utility during the past one or two decades. Conversion of dry latrines in a big way has made this community jobless to a large extent in the rural areas. Another important reason is that septic latrines are not very common in rural areas and people go to vacant spaces for easing themselves. Thus, no scavenging is required. This community had a long association with the bamboo work which they do now on a large scale as it gives them a livelihood throughout the year. The basket and winnowing fan which is used in marriage are made by them. They have almost a monopoly and no one from the other village is permitted to supply it as it comes under customary rights. Apart from bamboo work they have started working as agricultural labour especially in North Bihar. The mass migration of agricultural labour to Punjab and Haryana and to other ctities as coolie and rickshaw-puller has generated their demand in agriculture sector. In return for their agricultural labour they receive foodgrains and cash somewhat similar to what they used to get in customary rights while doing scavenging work. This shift of occupation from scavenging to agriculture has linked them directly to the rural economy of which they were never a part. This has given a new dimension to their customary rights. Definitely their demand as agricultural labour is eroding the stigma of untouchability attached to them.

This so-called unclean community no more keeps aloof from performing religious practices in their everyday life. Their religiosity has gone up. They observe almost every festival with zeal. During the festival of *Chhat* they use different *Ghat* (bank of a pond and river) to perform the festival. Visiting sacred places, especially Deoghar, is now common. They hang the pictures and posters of gods and goddesses in their houses. Since women are the carriers of tradition and are more religious, they are playing a major role in this transformation. Almost all religious rituals are performed by them. This evolution from nature worship to idol worship among the scavenger community is part of the process of sanskritisation. Migration is playing an important role in making them religious due to more contact with outer society. Many have stopped eating beef and lay great emphasis on vegetarianism. *Puja Karne Se Dukh Dur Hota Hai*, religion is panacea for all sorrows, it is the ideological thesis emerging in this community, which has travelled a long way to establish their identity in the Hindu cultural set-up, perhaps with the latent objective of being regarded as a clean community.

Large-size families which used to be the hallmark of the scavenger community have almost disappeared. It is replaced by the nuclear family system. The industrial urban system has also reduced the size of family. There are certain social and economic factors behind this. The individual goes from village to city in search of employment. On account of the constraints of limited wages and small accommodation, he is forced to follow the small family norm. Division of labour is strictly based on the earning ability of the family members. In case the female is earning more, all the domestic work like cooking and rearing of children is performed by the male. Despite the fact that the scavengers prefer nuclear family, they still remain attached emotionally with the family of orientation.

Scavengers are strictly an endogamous group but in the present decade incidence of inter-caste love marriage is increasing. These love marriages mainly take place in the scheduled caste category. Especially, those who are in Government service prefer to marry according to their choice as they can maintain their spouse on their own. Likewise, this economic independence has increased the dowry rate in this community. The earning capacity of a male determines his dowry. Dowry is paid both in cash and kind. Incidence of dowry torture is common in this community. In most of the cases it ends in separation. In case of torture, many times the local police and caste panchayat are consulted by the victim. The caste panchayat has been more successful than the other formal institutions in resolving such crises. Second marriage is also performed to get more dowry. In this community dowry has been adopted from the caste Hindus. Craze for material goods is the reason behind increase of dowry. They are not insulated from change taking place in their neighbourhood. Desire to have a radio, television and other consumer items provokes them to ask for dowry which also enhances their social status within and outside the community.

Divorce is resorted to if the wife does not get along well with her husband or *vice-versa*. The simplest way of divorce among the scavengers is when a wife goes and lives in her parental house and refuses to return to her husband's house even when asked to do so. This is a firm ground for divorce in this community.

In the sixties and seventies the scavengers were considered a blot on the society. Even animals were treated better than members of this community. In marriage or other social occasions, they were asked to eat the leftover along with the street dogs. This perception of caste Hindus has changed much in recent years and on some social occasions they are formally invited. Upper caste people now eat and drink along with scavengers. Youths in rural areas find the house of a scavenger convenient for drinking alcohol and country liquor. Scavengers have gradually changed their life-style. Women wear traditional but clean clothes and youths have adopted modern dress. Children of such scavenger families who are well-placed in cities very easily mix with the children of other communities and this inter-mixing is no more considered a taboo. Even the youths of scavenger community who are successful in their career are cited as an example for others by the villagers irrespective of their caste origin.

6. *Educated Urban Elite*

Dr. Sheo Prasad Gautam is a member of Bihar College Service Commission, Patna. He is a nominated member of the Senate of Bhagalpur and Patna University. Earlier he was a Reader in the Commerce Department of SRK Goenka College, Sitamarhi in B.R. Ambedkar Bihar University, Muzaffarpur. He was born in 1944 in Dhaobel Bazar in Baniyapur block of Saran district. He passed his Matriculation examination in 1961, B.Com. (Hons.) in 1965 and M.Com. in 1967.

His father was a labourer in Calcutta from his childhood. Dr. Gautam started working as a tutor. He got co-operation from villagers in his career building. There was not much of untouchability in the village. However, there was a separate well for drinking purposes for his family members. He has four sons and one daughter. The elder son has taken a degree in Civil Engineering and Computer Designing. The second son is an adhoc lecturer in the LSW Department of A.N. College, Patna. His third son has completed his M.Com. and is studying for B.Ed. His daughter is a student of Post-Graduate class in Geography in Patna University. The fourth son is a student of B.A. Part I in Sociology. His wife is a Supervisor in Telegraph Office, Patna.

Dr. Gautam took his Ph.D. in 1994 on 'The Role of Bihar State Co-operative Land Development Bank Ltd. in the Agricultural Development of Bihar (with special reference to Sitamarhi District)'. He has also guided one research scholar on 'The Role of Co-operative in Agricultural Finance of Bihar with special reference to Satamarhi District'.

During his student days he formed 'Mehtar Chhatra Kalyan Mahasabha'. In 1969 he became a member of All India Safai Mazdoor Congress. The anniversary of Shri Jagjivan Ram was organised but Ambedkar's anniversary had not been celebrated. Dr. Gautam organised first anniversary of Ambedkar during 1969. In 1972, he founded Pradeshik Ambedkar Samaj which is a registered organisation under Societies Registration Act 1860. He feels that scavenger community would get respect only by joining the mainstream. He had to work as a salesman in the village market. He got co-operation from Shri Deep Narayan Singh a veteran co-operative leader of the State. He formed Akhil Bharatiya Mehtar Mahasabha in October, 1998. The head office of this organisation is in Patna. He is going to organise a National Convention in the near future.

The exploitation of scavenging community was rampant in 1969. Even Municipal Supervisors became money-lenders. They used to charge high interest rate of 25% per month. They used to abuse and give threats to them. Similarly, local police used to collect commission from criminals of the Dom caste.

At that time labour laws were not followed by the Municipal Corporation. Gratuity and pension was not paid regularly at that time. Some educated persons are also engaged in this profession for a consideration. He has urged the scavenging community to take up other kinds of work and give up scavenging. Government should come forward to implement labour laws, abolish untouchability and ensure human rights by organising *Lok Adalat* and providing social justice to deprived classes.

Scavengers do not get other employment opportunities in the urban areas. The future of scavengers is bleak. Central and State Government officials do not take interest in the welfare of scavengers. Under the liberation of scavengers scheme some people have been trained but not rehabilitated. Some of the scavenger youth got three-wheelers but later they were seized and taken to the police station. The drivers did not have courage to go and get them back from the police station. According to him the Scheduled Caste Development Corporation is defunct. No development work is being implemented by this Corporation. He organised Mehtar Chhatra Kalyan Mahasabha during 1966-67. For the educational development of scavenger community he has motivated them. Being a member of Bihar College Service Commission he lamented that there is no applicant from the Mehtar community. The reason is lack of payment by the affiliated colleges. Their economic situation is so bad that they can not wait for this job. Other scheduled caste and backward caste candidates are larger in number. Hardly 7-8 candidates of scavenger community were appointed through Bihar College Service Commission.

No one from the scavenger community can start a tea-stall or vegetable shop due to untouchability. There is discrimination on the basis of caste. There is programme for SC/ST in the rural areas but there is no such programme for urban scavengers. There should be large-scale employment in the urban areas for the scavengers. He urged that a committee should decide whether those SC who are well-off and have already availed reservation scheme of Government should continue to enjoy it. He alleged that even Ministers belonging to scheduled castes have not done any good to the scavenger society. Dom, Musahar and Mehtar are still lagging behind. There should be a Safai Mazdoor Ayog in the State. The function of Safai Mazdoor Ayog would be to examine the status of scavengers in the municipal bodies. It will report to the Government. Thus, it will become a link between the Government and the employees. For political participation he advised that people from scavenger community should be nominated. No party is doing this. In Punjab, 50% of total reservation for scheduled castes is given to Majhabi Balmikis. Likewise Rajasthan Government is also planning to give 3% reservation to Balmikis. Similar action is contemplated in Maharashtra, Madhya Pradesh and Uttar Pradesh.

Suggestion for the Empowerment of Scavengers

1. There must be participation of scavengers in the local bodies.
2. There should be participation of scavengers as representatives in the high level committees of Welfare Development and others.
3. Political parties must give organisational work to the Balmikis. But this benefit should go to those persons who have interest in social work.
4. Safai Mazdoor Ayog (Safai Mazdoor Commission) should be constituted in each State.

7. *Resurgent Youth*

Shri Sikander Raut is at present working in the Patna Office of Sulabh International as a sweeper. He was only four months old when his father, a sweeper working on temporary basis at Patna Medical College and Hospital (PMCH), passed away. Later his mother joined the PMCH as a sweeper on compassionate grounds after a gap of five years. During these five years his mother along with his six elder sisters used to beg to survive. Four years back his mother retired and later died of cancer. After his mother's retirement, he along with his wife and son are living in a rented house. Grand-parents and other close relatives never gave any help during his bad days.

He attended school and passed seventh class examination. He had to give up his education due to poverty although his mother was willing to educate him. He took to the scavenging work at a very early age. Through one of his relatives who is already working at Sulabh International, he joined the Sulabh Organisation twelve years back. In his mid-twenties, he regards himself as fortunate as he is in a position to meet his family expenses. Some of his friends of the same age group are sitting idle. In Sulabh he has to do the sweeping work of the office and he is free to take up other means of earning in his spare time.

According to him untouchability has decreased in recent years but it has not vanished. Few people are ready to accept that scavengers are human beings. His own personal experience is not less painful. When he was only fifteen years old, unaware about the stigma attaching to his caste, along with other scavengers he was cleaning the chamber of a pourflush latrine at Patna. After the work was over, he went to take water from the tap fixed in the campus of the house. His touch of the tap made the owner of the house angry. He broke the tap with the help of an iron rod in his presence to show that it was now useless for him. Many years have gone by, but the message is still fresh for him. On many other occasions, similar experiences have been repeated, but now he finds himself prepared for it.

Leaders have a high position in our community. There is no other way to get any work done other than seeking help from local leader. Establishing a good rapport with the leader is not an easy task. Many times we have to follow them during rallies and bandhs. There are many leaders who have the dual responsibility of trade union and community. Ramji Neta is one of them. He is both a community leader and a trade union leader of PMCH where he works as a sweeper. During rallies and bandhs he collects scavengers from different parts of the city and arranges their participation. Though a Communist, he does not maintain distance from leaders of other parties. For other big leaders he works as a mediator to mobilise and influence voters at the time of election. Politics is a profitable profession for these leaders and changes their life-style overnight. Among the scavengers, very few have the desire for leadership and politics, and they normally do not participate in activities other than attending meetings and making casual calls on the house of their community leader. Political empowerment of the weaker section has been a vital agenda for almost all political parties. Despite government efforts, scavengers are afraid to vote and they mostly keep away from a polling booth. Those who dare to exercise their right fail to do so due to bogus voting. The phenomenon of bogus voting is not new but has increased in recent decades. Denial of their voting right further alienates them from participating in the political process. They feel that the elected legislator does not care for them, as they do not cast the vote.

Education can play a vital role in reshaping the future of the children. He wishes to educate his only son so that he can shape a future of his own, something which he himself missed in his childhood. Any job apart from scavenging is his life-dream for his son. He gives priority to clerical job in Government offices and banks for his son. His wife who hails from a family still engaged in scavenging has also a similar wish. She gave up the profession of scavenging after her marriage and is a full-time housewife concentrating more on the education of her son.

The scavenger community is very compartmentalised and insulated from the wider society. Lack of proper education and low level of aspiration hampers their chance to come out of the cocoon. It is not always that they are ill-treated by other members of the society. At the same time their own thinking restricts interaction with others. There are many examples including his own in the community who have at last get rid of this degrading profession. This requires personal effort to give up traditional occupation, but on the contrary most of the young scavengers are homesick and seldom wish to go out for other jobs. In urban areas there is more chance for interaction as well as job mobility. Personal performance and a desire to perform better can definitely change the course of the youths if they aspire for it. Family support and personal qualities are the foremost prerequisites. In his own case after getting rid of scavenging and joining Sulabh International, he now plans to get any class IV job in government department. He is satisfied with the present nature of work but wishes to get more salary and facility like free house etc., if he gets any government job suiting his education and work experience.

The government is ineffective to tackle the scavengers' problem. Most of the advantages go to the other scheduled castes. The Indira Awas Yojana may benefit the scavengers. The public distribution system also does not cover them. The government officials do not show favour to them. For all work they have to pay them. In most of the cases the payment is made through their leader who acts as a mediator.

Life-style of the scavengers specially the youths has changed a lot in recent years. They now put on modern dresses and try to look different from their traditional images. The mode of entertainment has also changed and now they prefer movies in cinema halls. Love and inter-caste marriage is now socially approved. Vegetables and pulses figure in their food.

Youths are not interested in the upliftment of their community. Lack of interest is also due to their lack of knowledge and social upbringing. Meetings are held only when someone from outside takes the initiative. In urban areas the community solidarity is slowly withering. People of older generation do not pay much attention to the cause of the community and they never try to form any organisation for such purposes. Individual interests count more. This is the main reason for their inability to reach the desired collective goals.

Problem-Oriented Case Studies

8. *Indebtedness*

Indebtedness is a common phenomenon in the scavenger community. Scarce resources and social expenditure along with addiction to drinks lands them at the doors of money-lenders who never fail to exploit their necessity. This vicious cycle of indebtedness and poverty has become a way of life among scavengers.

On the whole, 71.46% of the scavengers are in debt out of the total 2450 scavengers covered under the study. Incomewise, the maximum number of cases of indebtedness is reported in the income group of below Rs. 2000 and Rs. 2001 to 4000 in all the rural and urban categories.

Table 11.3: Showing Sex and Residential Category-wise Distribution of Debtors

Category	Sex					
	Male		Female		Total	
Urban						
More than one lakh	412	(56.43)	318	(43.56)	730	(73.00)
50,000 to one lakh	214	(52.45)	194	(47.54)	408	(68.00)
20,000 to 50,000	75	(64.65)	41	(35.34)	116	(58.00)
Below 20,000	75	(54.74)	62	(45.25)	137	(68.05)
Total	776	(55.78)	615	(44.21)	1391	(69.55)
Rural	190	(52.77)	170	(47.22)	360	(80.00)
All	966	(54.88)	785	(44.83)	1751	(71.46)

Sources for loan are many but the scavengers have more access to private money-lenders (93.77%). Official agencies like banks and Scheduled Caste Finance Corporation had benefited only 0.05% of the scavengers. The role of NGOs in providing loan to the scavengers is also negligible as they have benefited only 0.11% of the scavengers.

In the absence of formal agencies providing loan to the needy scavengers, the non-formal agencies have a major stake in this nefarious business. Apart from traditional non-formal agents like Mahajans and Pathans, the emerging elite in the scavenger community also lend money to other members of the community. An instance of this is Smt. Leela Devi of Purnea. She is not only in the staff of the local Municipal Corporation but is also the Secretary of the local scavengers union. She uses her clout of being the Secretary to influence the officials of the Corporation to work as money-lender without any fear or danger. She gives loans to the needy and takes the interest on every salary day. The interest rate charged by her is between 20% to 30% per month, somewhat similar to other money-lenders.

Generally, loans are provided on a flat interest rate of 20% to 30% per month, depending on the urgency of the need. As there are no formal agencies from which they can obtain loan, the informal sources like Mahajans, Pathans, etc., are free to charge exorbitant rate of interest from the needy. These money-lenders find it easy and more convenient to take the repayment on monthly basis, at least the interest amount due to two reasons : (i) it is easy for the scavengers to repay a small sum which will otherwise add up into a bigger amount, (ii) the money-lenders do not want to take the risk as there is chance of scavengers' eviction. There is a fixed system in vogue among the money-lenders to take back their money. On every salary day they contact the Municipal Corporation/Nigam Office. They are hands-in-glove with the clerical staff of the office who help them extract their interest amount from the salary. Consent of the indebted scavenger is not necessary in the whole process and he remains a silent spectator. For their help the Municipal Office staff are also compensated in cash and kind. On the other hand, scavengers also find it easier to pay back the amount on monthly basis. Since the money-lenders are only interested in their monthly interest, not in capital repayments, they also target the payment of interest on the monthly basis and debtors continue to remain in debt all the time. When the scavengers are unable to return the loan they resort to dishonest and unscrupulous means. This behaviour compels them to mortgage the house and ornaments and other belongings.

The members of the scavenger community indulge in wasteful expenditure on social and religious functions, like birth, marriage and death. They have to spend a good deal of money on various items connected with these ceremonies. Marriage dinner, which no scavenger family can avoid, is a costly affair. Prevalence of dowry and its gradual increase in their society has a definite relationship with incurring debt. Money-lenders lend the money on this occasion as it gives them professional credibility. Celebrating birth of a new child and house construction are other important reasons in addition to borrowing money for death, disease, gambling, liquor and litigation.

Loans are rarely taken for productive purposes. Most loans are non-productive loans. Scavengers are keen to take loan to indulge in 'Matka' or 'Single Digit Lottery' as it is locally known. These lotteries are unadulterated gambling. There is a daily draw and the results are conveyed within minutes to various stalls through STD. The scavengers think that in these lotteries they have equal chance to win something, unlike in other things. Buying the tickets in the morning and waiting for the result till evening not only keeps them away from job, but it also makes them pathetic and hostile in the end when they lose it. The lure of easy money from lottery to fulfil their dreams is also attracting the fair sex and the children. Moneylenders keep a close vigil on the whole process of the lottery and the position of their client, who requires more money to gamble and who is in a position to return the money.

Since majority of the families are in the salaried services in the Municipal Corporation/Nigam, they find it difficult to balance their budget. Limited salaried income, sometimes supplemented by various other subsidiary occupations, is found to be insufficient to make both ends meet. Non-payment of salary on time has been a major cause for borrowing money. In recent years the situation has become from bad to worst. Before the financial year 1991-92, the Municipal Corporation/Nigam had to contribute only 25% of the annual budget from its own revenue. The rest 75% of the amount was met by the State Government. After the financial year 1991-92, the local body is no more supported by the State Government. The local body is unable to meet this situation and the salaries are not paid on time. In most of the cases they are in arrears for many months after which it is released in instalments. Regular transfer of the officials concerned with the policy making of the Corporation/ Nigam hampers the revenue collection on which payment of salaries of scavengers depends.

The complex situation of indebtedness is not limited to one generation. Debt is inherited by the son if his father fails to repay it before his death. This obnoxious practice among the scavengers goes from generation to generation. Very few are there to question the validity of this practice as to why he will repay the debt which his father had taken for the reasons not known to him. In cases of refusal, the money-lenders seek the help of local police and goondas. The role of police in giving assistance to these money-lenders is questionable as the money-lenders do not have any formal licence for carrying on this trade. This way or the other, it is the money-lenders who have the final say. Willingly or unwillingly a scanvenger has to repay the debt which his parents had taken not only for the continuance of this system but also to prove his own personal ability and honesty to repay the debt so that in future he can obtain a loan.

Janam Se Kafan Tak Udhar Laga Rahata Hai is a very simple description of the scavengers' fate. It seems that the prospect of a loan-free society is a distant dream. On the contrary, the scavenger society is becoming more loan-based due to multiple reasons. The adoption of consumerist culture, putting more emphasis on the material goods, has made great impact on this community which otherwise was habitualised to living within their limited means. In the urban society scavengers are likely to adopt the life-styles of their neighbourhood, which in most of the cases forces them to take more loan.

9. *Drunkenness*

A large percentage of scavengers of both the sexes are addicted to drink. They consume toddy as well as spiritous liquor and it has become a part of their way of life. It has many adverse effects, economic as well as social. Rise in income does not necessarily raise their standard of living and it invariably leads to indebtedness. Family as an institution loses its sanctity due to constant quarrel between the husband and the wife. Children become vagrants and do not go to school. Their own efficiency deteriorates. In short, these factors depress the quality of life of the scavengers in a big way.

On the whole 93.79% of the scavengers covered in this study consume alcohol. Of this, 55.33% are males and 44.69% are females. In rural areas about 99.98% scavengers are habituated to drinks as compared to 93.79% in urban areas.

Table 11.4: Showing Sexwise Break-up of Scavengers taking Alcohol in Different Categories

Sex	Categories		Urban		Rural	Total
	A	B	C	D		
Male	507 (55.89)	295 (52.21)	121 (66.21)	109 (55.32)	239 (53.58)	1271 (55.30)
Female	400 (44.10)	270 (47.78)	62 (33.87)	88 (44.67)	207 (46.41)	1027 (44.69)
All	907 (90.70)	565 (94.17)	183 (91.50)	197 (98.50)	446 (99.98)	2298 (93.79)

Income-groupwise, in the income group of Rs. 6,000 and above, on an average both males and females spend about 7% of their monthly income on drinks, whereas, in the income group of below Rs. 2,000, 12.24% and 11.66% of the income is spent by the men and women respondents respectively. The most disturbing revelation is that in all the categories, females spend as much as males on drinks.

It has been noticed that females are more prone to drink in the community where they work more outside the family. Women who are earning can be more useful to the family if they keep away from drink. Her love for drinks does strain othe economy of the family. Indebtedness and drinking are closely related and in communities where drinking is rampant among the females, the budget of the family is destabilised. In some cases the money-lenders exploit the women in many ways.

The quality of life of the scavengers is very poor. Among other reasons, alcoholism is very important. Being engaged in an unclean profession and keen to forget the day-to-day problems forces them to drink. The nature of work, isolation from the mainstream society, and lower standard of living are some of the other reasons advanced by the scavengers for their addiction to drink. For them there is no way for their survival and recreation other than consumption of alcohol. It seems that alcohol is used as a cover for their petty squabbles within and outside the family in their daily life. *Pine Ke Bad To Larai Jhagra Laga Rahta Hai*. This is not only due to intoxication, rather it has almost become a norm in their culture. The social control mechanism is ineffective. Institutions which regulate the community fail to restrict the alcohol intake and its consequences. With the growth of urbanisation, the mass migration of the scavengers and the anonymity in urban areas makes them miserable drink addicts. Likewise, in the urban areas the youths are very fond of imitating the western culture in their neighbourhood where *Charas*, *Ganja* and *Bhang* are taken frequently. They learn this culture from their peers in slums where they live and grow.

Drinking affects the scavengers socially, physically and economically. Excess drinking leads to individual disorganisation resulting in abnormal and unhealthy social relationship. The alcoholic forsakes his home, his family and his profession. Drink also contributes to creation of family tensions. But today this friction has been greatly increased by drinking among women and therefore, family disorganisation has accelerated. A strong addiction to drink on the part of the husband or wife is a constant source of friction in the family and leads to breakup. When women find that children are subjected to the vagaries of an alcoholic father, they often resort to divorce. In certain families where people have neither the knowledge of law nor the resources for divorce, drunkenness often causes untold misery. The family retains its structure but the normal cohesion is completely shaken. Drinking of cheap and county-made liquor makes a person physically weak and affects the brain. He gradually loses his mental balance and in most of the cases he becomes violent. Besides these manifest problems, resistance to all diseases is appreciably lowered by heavy and regular consumption of liquor. Scavengers who are having a very tight budget to meet their basic needs face many hardships in case a large amount is spent on this social vice. Wife and children suffer more in certain circumstances. Children are forced to act as child labour and are kept away from school. Females are left with no other option but to take up other work for meeting their daily household expenditure.

To check the extent of alcoholism certain preventive measures are suggested as under :

(a) Campaign should be organised for this propaganda. Some people should educate the public through all existing social organisations which have experience of this kind of work. Among them may be included temperance associations, local leaders, women's associations, trade unions, religious and cultural organisations, etc. The Education Department may educate students and youths. Press should be fully utilised to rally public opinion around prohibition.

(b) Women's associations can bring a sea-change by imitating the model of Andhra Pradesh and Haryana if they work in a mission-oriented manner. What they lack is the basic orientation for the same. Non-government agencies can play a vital role in developing missionary zeal in them to take up this cause.

(c) Propaganda against drinking should include women as it affects them most. They are responsible for running the family and upbringing of their children with meagre income. Addiction to alcohol spoils the future of women and children and eventually it ruins the family.

(d) Recreation centres should be established on a large scale both by the States and NGOs. The Municipal Corporation/ Nigam should encourage the formation of a club for its staff. Some experiments of this sort have proved beneficial. A scavengers' club established by Muzaffarpur Municipal Corporation under the guidance of Mr. K.K. Pathak, Administrator, keeps the scavengers engaged in the club after their working hours. This approach will limit their level of drinking. This can be extended to their residential locality also by making a community hall with television facility for their family members.

(e) It is of utmost importance to keep in touch with the families of habitual takers of alcohol. Though drunkards offer hard resistance to persuation, social workers must not give up. Both government and the NGOs can coordinate their activities in this direction. Although many NGOs are working in this field, the coverage of scavengers under their programme is very low. Therefore, an effort should be made to cover maximum number of scavengers under their programme.

(f) Certain other drinks like tea, cold drinks, etc., should be encouraged in place of alcohol. This can reduce the extent of drinking.

12

OVERVIEW AND AGENDA FOR FUTURE ACTION

There is some controversy on the definition of the scavengers. Whether the parameter should be the caste or occupation, has yet not been settled. In the caste model of social stratification the fifth group is constituted by outcastes or untouchables. These untouchables are regarded as unclean, base and impure and perform unclean and degrading tasks including disposal of nightsoil and scavenging. Another perspective is that scavengers are a functional community recruited from different social groups performing this occupation and are at the bottom of the caste hierarchy due to multiple reasons. The caste model of social stratification is confined within the Hindu worldview, whereas, the scavenger as a functional category is free from any restriction. In the present study the latter model has been used to locate the scavengers. Thus, the scavenger is one who himself is or his forefathers were partially or wholly engaged in the obnoxious and inhuman occupation of manually removing nightsoil and filth.

The present study is based on the figures of Planning Commission's report of 1989. As there has been no further survey conducted, and there is fast occupational mobility in this community the numbers may be going down each year. This is due to conversion of dry latrines into pourflush latrines in most towns. In the absence of a census survey of this community we have to depend on this decade-old figure.

The issues related to scavengers and scavenging have been raised broadly under four objectives in the present study, *viz*., (i) to explore the living and working condition of the scavengers and the impact of various welfare programmes meant for their liberation and total development; (ii) to bring scavengers from the margin to the mainstream of the Indian society through abolition of discriminatory attitudes and values apart from discussing the implications of the changing scenario from the point of view of human rights; (iii) to probe the gender differences in scavenging and to suggest ways and means to empower this community; and (iv) to find out reasons for the tardy implmentation of the recommendations of Committees and Commissions appointed for this purpose.

The bulk of the scavengers are in the age group of 36-50 years. In both urban and rural areas majority of the scavengers are married. There were no Sikh and Christian scavengers in the surveyed area. Only Hindu and Muslim scavengers were found. Castewise, Mehtar and Dom were in majority. Most of the scavengers preferred nuclear family. The average family consists of 6-8 members. The average income range of most of the scavenger families is from Rs. 4,001 to Rs. 6,000 per month. In urban areas most of the scavengers live in rented houses. Very few reside in the quarters provided by the Corporation. The condition of these quarters is very bad and they may crumble very soon. Filth and garbage around the houses of scavengers produce foul smell.

Taps and handpumps provide drinking water to the scavengers. Even this facility is not uniform and in many places there is scarcity of drinking water. The drinage is bad in the localities where scavengers reside. The drains are often used by the children for defecation. In the urban area scavengers have more individual toilets while there is no such toilet in the rural area. Further, there is either no arrangement of toilets or the condition of the toilet was bad in most of the towns as the Municipal Corporations have no funds for maintenance.

More than half of the sample scavenger families do not have electricity in their houses. It was found that scavengers in the higher income group in the urban area avail this facility mainly through their own efforts.

Most of the scavengers, both in the urban and rural areas, go for private medical care like private nursing home, quacks and registered medical practitioners. Very few visit Government hospital as P.H.C. doctors and other health workers in Government medical institutions are found absent and they charge fees for their services.

Most of the scavengers, both men and women, are engaged in subsidiary occupations like basket making, toy making, rag picking and carrying of bricks and other manual work including the work of agricultural labour. Some scavengers in North Bihar have now become agricultural labour. They have taken full advantage of the huge migration of the traditional agricultural labour to other States like Punjab, Haryana, etc. Their working as agricultural labour has also elevated their social status and they are not considered as polluting any more. Due to the shrinking of their traditional occupation, the scavengers are compelled to take up supplementary work for their livelihood. Another reason is that majority of the municipal authorities and notified area committees do not regularly pay salary to their staff. Sometimes it is in arrears for months together. In urban area most of the scavengers earn upto Rs. 500 from the supplementary work whereas in rural area such income is larger.

Indebtedness is endemic among the scavengers and most of them its victims. It is common in the urban as well as rural areas. The main reason behind indebtedness is unemployment, poverty and irregular payment of salary by the municipal authorities. The other reasons are gambling, alcoholism and expenditure on social obligations like marriage, death and medicine. Sometimes they have to mortgage their beddings, boxes, utensils and even wearing clothes for meeting their basic requirements like food.

The saving tendency is more in the scavengers of the urban area in comparison to rural area. Due to low level of income in the rural area the propensity to save is low. Similarly, the tendency towards saving among the females was more in comparison with male respondents. Among the males, in the urban area their saving tendency was more than in rural area. The reason behind more saving in the urban area was that scavengers have higher income level in comparison to rural respondents. In rural areas people are poor and unemployed and they have no regular source of income.

So far as rural-urban employment differential is concerned, a large number of permanent jobs for the scavengers are available in the urban area while they are limited in the rural area. Majority of scavengers in the cities having more than one lakh population have a permanent job. This percentage declines in other categories and in rural areas. Small towns and rural areas have more temporary staff while large cities have more permanent staff. This illustrates the nature of employment of the scavengers.

Television and radio as the means of entertainment are very common in urban and rural areas. These sources of entertainment not only entertain them but at the same time they make them aware about developments taking places in the neighbourhood and in the country at large.

Scavengers have close relationship with people outside their caste. It is seen more in the urban area in comparison to the rural area. In the rural area the stigma of their caste haunts them and it affects their day-to-day life. In the urban area due to greater social mobility and high degree of social participation they are able to come closer to the people outside their caste.

The jajmani system in customary rights has started withering away under the impact of new economic forces, mass migration, urbanisation, the emergence of salaried and wage-earning groups and the monetisation of the economy. Customary rights are only found among the scavengers in some pockets. There have been substantial changes in the working and payment patterns.

The status of women scavengers is comparatively higher than among other such communities. This undermines male hegemony. Due to their earning ability women are free to remarry after separation if the situation demands. Despite the fact that women in this community enjoy greater authority and respect, the attitude towards educating the female children is still negative. Boys are sent to school while girls join their mothers at work at an early age. Most of the scavengers are of the opinion that there is no need to waste money on girls' education.

Head-loading is still in vogue and most of the head-loaders are women. Despite all the efforts by the Government and the NGOs, this curse is still persisting. It certainly affects the status of women in and outside the community. It has been noticed that the main reason for this is the tacit acquiescence of women to continue in the caste occupation.

In view of these conditions scavengers continue to constitute the most disadvantaged section of the population, socially, educationally and economically. Their social degradation, oppression and exploitation have been ubiquitous and a persistent social reality. Numerous Commissions and Committees were constituted, both at the National and State levels, yet most of these have largely concerned themselves with scavengers employed by civic bodies. On the other hand, the malaise of manual scavenging is much more extensive and deep-seated. It is hardly surprising that whatever policies and programmes have been made for them have managed to touch, at best, the fringe of the problem.

Despite the conversion of dry latrines into water closets, the degrading practice of manual scavenging survives as the state authorities have relied too much on the letter of the law. Local government has remained indifferent towards sanitation and disposal of nightsoil. Apart from social degradation, they are exposed to occupational hazards and suffer from numerous physical impairments and ailments. Their literacy, education and skill development is low, resulting in under-representation in prestigious and remunerative occupations, further making their participation in development programmes nominal, if not negligible.

Agenda for Action

The present study has brought out in bold relief various aspects of life and work among scavengers. Standing on the threshold of the third millennium, the scavenger scenario is a total shame. In spite of the declared intention of the government, provision of funds and the work of voluntary agencies, the pace of development in respect of the scavengers has been remarkably slow. In course of our study the reasons for this have been given at various places. It is now time to suggest ways and means by which the scavenger society can join the mainstream by shedding their demeaning profession, avail human rights to the fullest extent and participate in the social life of the community, contributing to its all-round development to the best of their ability.

Till the time that manual scavenging continues scavengers should be provided with gloves, gumboots, scrapers, shovels and wheel-barrows. Head-loading should be totally forbidden. Punitive measures should be taken against municipal authorities infringing these orders. However, it has been realised that the salvation of the scavengers lies in the speedy conversion of dry latrines into pourflush latrines for which inexpensive technology has been devised, tested and popularised by the Sulabh International during the last three decades, not only in different parts of India but also in several other countries. This entails speedy action on two fronts. More funds should be earmarked by the government for setting up sanitary complexes both in rural and urban areas. The well-to-do section of the society should be encouraged to convert their toilets by giving them a small subsidy. In rural areas those who can afford would certainly construct improved toilets in their houses. For those who cannot do so, community toilets have to be set up by the efforts of Panchayati Raj institutions. Construction of individual toilets should be considered as primary duty of individuals and local bodies, since neglect on their part will constitute a grave health hazard. In fact, the sanitary aspect should be emphasised in any health education programme. People's organisations must see that maximum funds are provided for this and the target fixed for this purpose is achieved on time. This would require more sincerity on the part of the implementing agency. Even institutions specially set up for the welfare of the scheduled caste communities do not give any priority to this work. Plans should be drawn up by such agencies for converting the rural and urban areas in different phases.

From time to time, seminars, workshops and competitions should be organised in different areas to review the progress of this work and to suggest any mid-term revision of policy and programmes in this context. In all the gatherings enlightened members of the scavenger society should be intimately involved.

Once the conversion of dry latrines and setting up of community toilets catches speed, the problem of rehabilitation of scavengers who have been displaced from the profession needs to be addressed. This can only be done by providing them alternative skills for making a living. The training programmes envisaged should work with the cafeteria approach and different kinds of trades be offered for training. These training centres should arrange for placement of trainees either in jobs or by helping them set up their own business with the financial support of banks or other lending agencies. There should be a regular machinery for monitoring training schemes and the follow-up of rehabilitation programmes. In each of these committees enlightened Bhangi leaders should also be included.

The study has brought out that indebtedness is a perpetual problem with them. They are born in debt, live in debt and die in debt. This phenomenon is the result of their chronic deficit household budget, their lack of foresight for unseen expenditure caused by illness, inability to curb social expenditure at the time of birth, marriage and death in the family and also by addiction to drinks. Each of these causes of indebtedness has to be looked into. There should be some provision for non-productive consumption loan in the lending agencies. Unless this is done the scavengers would continue to remain in the stranglehold of rapacious money-lenders.

The study has revealed that the payment of salary to the scavengers is always in arrears. Thus, the municipal authorities by their action are throwing the scavengers into the jaws of money-lenders. It is, therefore, of utmost importance that payment of salaries to Bhangis is regularised in the shortest possible time. It has been observed that in some cases the municipal staff is hands-in-glove with the money-lenders. Severe punishment should be meted/ out to such municipal staff.

Addiction to drugs and drinks is also a common feature of the life of scavengers in Bihar. A large number of scavengers, some of them very young, have been found addicted to drugs of various types. Some of them want to make fortune through lotteries and 'Matka'. A substantial amount of hard earned money is being spent through these. Besides this a large number of scavengers are addicted to hard drinks. A large amount of money is spent over this. It is also seen that not only men but women also are drink addicts. While drinks exhilarate body mechanism temporarily, they ultimately act as a debilitating factor and may lead to serious ailments. Other aspects of the drink syndrome perhaps are more obnoxious. Drinks lead to brawls in the family and between families. This tells upon children. Otherwise also, children suffer because resources which would have gone for their clothing, health and education are drained elsewhere. It is, therefore, necessary that effective temperance programmes should be mounted in scavenger locations so that drink habit goes down gradually. Women can take a lead in this direction because it is they who bear the brunt of this social evil. This is indeed a difficult task but it can be facilitated with valuable inputs through both print and non-print media, through skits and plays which would make a lasting impact on the people.

One of the factors which has restricted the occupational shift of the scavengers is the near-absence of education among them. The percentage of literacy is below 10%. Among women it is much lower. The enrolment of scavenger children in schools is very low. It is, therefore, necessary that speedy steps be taken to educate the children. This will enable them to diversify their occupation and to seek employment or take up some kind of self-employment or petty business for making a living. Thus, the training and rehabilitation programmes would not be necessary beyond the present generation. It is seen that the educated sections of scavengers society have joined the mainstream and are participating in all social activities. More non-formal education centres should be started in Bhangi locations. In this context special efforts have to be made to bring the girls under the educational net. The apathy of scavenger parents towards the education of the girl child has to be overcome. If necessary, some incentives should be provided for it. Education of the girl child would go a long way in raising the quality of life of the entire community.

It is an anachronism that the scavengers who have the responsibility of keeping the environment clean, right from the toilets to drains and streets, themselves remain in dirt and squalor. This is partly due to their dilapidated houses and residential locations as well as to their lack of awareness about clean healthy living. It is, therefore, necessary that sanitation and health awareness programmes must be stepped up among them.

Although the scavengers are at the bottom of Indian society not many NGOs have been attracted to take up programmes for their well-being. Gandhiji's love for the *Bhangis* has not been emulated by most voluntary organisations. In fact, Antyodaya programmes should have been taken up among them. The Sulabh International Social Service Organisation has slowly built up a movement in the country under the innovative and inspiring leadership of Dr. Bindeshwar Pathak for the emancipation of the scavengers from their present state and given them hope for a new life based on human dignity and social justice, through various programmes of training and rehabilitation, education, health and adoption of Bhangi families by members of upper caste. The problem is so vast in its magnitude that only one organisation cannot do so. Even at the State level, it is necessary that more NGOs should come up and devote themselves whole-heartedly to this task. There is no dearth of money for such causes. The Sulabh Movement has shown the way and acted as a catalyst. The Valmiki leadership has not made any efforts to set up NGOs for this work. Pressure for this work should be built up from below. The Valmiki youth are so much engrossed in the ordinary business of life that they do not find time to make efforts for the development of their community.

Although the government at the Central and State level is committed to the liberation and rehabilitation of scavengers and their joining the mainstream of society, the functioning of the institutions and organisations devised for this purpose is not up to the mark. The National Commission for Scheduled Castes and Scheduled Tribes has not taken any interest and initiative in this regard. The National Commission for Safai Karamcharis set up in 1994 and reconstituted in 1997 does not seem to have taken off. At the State level the Department of Urban Development and the Public Health Engineering Department have not been able to spend the funds allocated for it during the Five-year Plans. Their apathy in the conversion of toilets and in the building of community toilets has slowed down the programmes of the liberation of scavengers. The same is the case with the non-utilisation of funds meant for their training and rehabilitation. The Scheduled Castes Co-operative Development Corporation has also failed in accelerating the programmes for the well-being of the scavengers. The activities of all the organisations dealing with the scavengers have to be effectively monitored so that they deliver the services expected of them at the right time. From time to time, conferences and seminars should be held to take note of the difficulties and problems experienced in the implementation of the welfare measures. These problems should be solved either by executive action or by mid-term revision of programmes and policies of the government. Such meetings should also take account of the co-ordination of the activities of different departments engaged in this task and also devise ways in which the NGOs could supplement and co-operate with state action if so required.

It has been widely recognised lately that development of the deprived and under-privileged communities depends largely on the political will of the State. This political will is determined by the clout wielded by the affected communities. Since the scavengers are a very small community it is but natural that such clout is non-existent. Even among the scheduled castes the scavengers are not able to pull their weight. They are not concentrated in any particular area from which they can expect to be elected to legislative or other bodies or enter corridors of power. It is only rarely that they are elected to either the Parliament or State Assembly. Even in those places that are reserved for scheduled castes in legislative bodies or government posts or in admissions to schools and colleges or grant of scholarships or stipends, they lose out to more populous and advanced scheduled castes. In political parties they do not figure as important functionaries. This is largely because of their poor political participation. Very few members of this community can spare time for political participation. At best, they end up as sub-leaders of scheduled caste leaders in factions of different political parties. From time to time, they have formed organisations which are short-lived as they always suffer from lack of resources, both human and material. Those who have gone up as high achievers in scavenger society are indeed examples of courage and perseverance but they have failed to enthuse their brethren to take up community welfare work. Corporate efforts by scavenger youth for development of the community are necessary to build up pressure from below.

One way to speed up the empowerment of the scavengers is to provide them protective discrimination on a preferential basis among scheduled castes. This can be done by bifurcating the list of scheduled castes in Bihar into two categories, one comprising the more populous and advanced castes like the Chamar, Dusadh, Pasi, Dhobi, etc., and the other comprising the Musahar, Mehtar, Dom, Lalbegi, Halalkhor etc., who are much less developed and have not been able to avail the benefits of reservation to an appreciable extent. Such an exercise has already been done in Haryana and Andhra Pradesh and has produced good results. The principle of grading of backwardness has already been accepted in the case of backward castes. There is no reason why it cannot be extended to the scheduled castes in Bihar.

We need to remind ourselves about the Father of the Nation's commitment to the development of the Bhangis or scavengers and his desire to be reborn as a Bhangi if he had a rebirth. This has connection to his concept of Antyodaya or development of the lowest rung of the society. We owe it to the Father of the Nation to complete his task with empathy, sincerity and devotion. The scavengers are not the concern of a department of the Government or of this commission or that. They are the concern of the entire Indian society, the nation at large. Let us, therefore, all combine our mite to complete this stupendous and unfinished task.

ANNEXURES

ANNEXURE—A

ETHNOGRAPHIC NOTES ON SCAVENGER CASTES IN BIHAR*

Balmiki

Some sections of a cluster of communities like the Bhangi, Mehtar, Lalbegi and other castes who were associated with scavenging in the past, who are now united as one community, claim common descent from the legendary saint Balmiki. There had been continuous migration of the present-day Balmikis from rural areas to towns and cities, but there had been no mass migration.

Female shawls, male turbans and tattoo marks had been their identification marks in the past, but they are no longer in vogue among the younger generation. Their total population in Uttar Pradesh, according to the 1981 census, is 7,44,821. They are predominately found in the rural areas. However, a good number of them *i.e.* 2,71,801 persons (36.49% of their total population) are returned from the urban areas. They are non-vegetarian and their staple diet includes wheat, rice and pulses like tur and urad. Mustard oil is the cooking medium. They occasionally consume alcoholic drinks.

The Balmiki are divided into various sub-castes and exogamous lineages. They regard themselves as Sudra. Sub-caste endogamy and lineage exogamy are the marriage rules. Adult marriage and

**Source* : Singh, K.S., *The Scheduled Caste,* Vol. II, Oxford University Press, New Delhi, 1995.

monogamy are prevalent and most marriages are negotiated. Vermilion, finger-rings, toe-rings and nose-pins are the marriage symbols for women. Dowry is paid in cash and kind. Residence after marriage is patrilocal. Divorce is not allowed. Families are most often nuclear in nature. Property passes from father to sons and the eldest son inherits the office and titles that were held by his father. Women have specific roles in economic, social and ritual spheres and in family management. They observe Hindu rituals on occasions like birth, mundan, marriage and death. Birth pollution is observed. The marriage rituals are performed at the bride's place and her parents host the marriage feast. The marriage is consummated at the groom's residence. They cremate their dead and dispose of the mortal remains in holy waters. Death pollution is observed.

The Balmiki have been associated with scavenging in the past. Now a good number of them serve as sweepers in public and private sector establishments. They have shifted from serving some households on a contract basis to being in regular service. According to the 1981 census, 29.90% of them are returned as workers (47.76% males and 9.65% females). A major proportion of the workers *i.e.* 41.88% are returned under 'other services' which probably indicates their involvement in their traditional occupation. However, a change from their traditional occupation to the primary section of economy is noticed, with 29.42% of the workers returned as agricultural labourers and 12.26% as cultivators. A small number, 3.70% are engaged in livestock, forestry etc., 4.54% in household industry and the remaining 8.20% workers are in various other services. Their community council (panchayat) maintains social control. The Balmiki are Hindus and their sacred specialists are the Brahmins. On occasions, their own community member also conducts different ritual observances connected with birth, marriage and death. Balmiki Jayanti is an important festival for them. This annual congregation strengthens the Balmiki socio-religious movement.

The Balmikis accept water, and kachcha and pucca food from all other communities with whom they interact. They share wells, water sources and crematoria with other communities. They have economic ties with other communities who they serve on a regular basis or occasionally. There are some who hold white-collar jobs. Political leadership has emerged among them at the regional level.

Balmiki favour formal education for their boys and girls, who study up to graduate and post-graduate levels depending upon the individual aptitude and circumstantial constraints. Their literacy rate, according to the 1981 census, is 4.90%. They favour and make use of modern and traditional medicare. Family planning is preferred and generally their women get sterilised. They are exposed to mass media and utilise communication, transport and postal facilities. Thcy avail of ration facilities and supplies.

Bansphor

Also known as the Benbansi-Bansphor, they consider themselves one of the sub-groups of the Doms. The term bansphors is derived from the Hindi word *bans* meaning bamboo and *phorna* mcaning to split. Some of them claim descent from the Ben-raja; yet another version is that they are descendants of Supat Bhagat. Crooke (1896) states that "Bansphore—a sub-caste of Doms may be considered separately as they have been separately enumerated at the last census". Their immigration from the west is said to have commenced some four generations ago and it still continues. In Gorakhpur they have a story that they are the descendants of Supat Bhagat who was a votary of Ramachandra. Risley (1891) describes them as "a sub-caste of Patnis in Bengal, sub-caste of Doms in Bihar who are mat and basket makers and do not remove filth". They are predominately distributed in rural areas. Bhojpuri, an Indo-Aryan language, is spoken among themselves while Hindi is spoken with others. The Devanagri script is used for written communication. They are non-vegetarian and their staple diet includes rice, wheat, maize, pulses, like tur, peas, beans and vegetables. Males regularly consume liquor but females do so only occasionally.

The Bansphors are aware of the varna system and place themselves in the Sudra category. They are endogamous but exogomy is maintained between the relative within four ascending generations on both the father's and the mother's side. Child marriages are followed by the '*gaona*' ceremony, and are usually settled through negotiation. Monogamy is the norm. Vermilion and toe-rings are the symbols of marriage for women. Bride price is paid in cash but dowry is paid both in cash and kind. The rule of residence is patrilocal. Divorce is permissible on grounds of barrenness, maladjustment or adultery. Remarriage is permissible. The common family types are nuclear and mixed extended, while property is equally inherited by all the sons, it is the eldest son who succeeds to the authority of the father. In addition to their household jobs, the women have important roles in the social, economic and religious spheres of life. They contribute to the family income and control family expenditure. Certain pre-delivery and post-delivery rituals are observed. Birth pollution is observed for twelve days. Marriage rituals are performed at the bride's place and marriage feasts are arranged by both the sides. The consummation of marriage takes place at the groom's residence. Death pollution is observed for twelve days. The dead are cremated and their mortal remains are disposed of in water.

Basketry is their traditional as well as present occupation. They are also involved in various other occupations, like agricultural labour, business, services, etc. According to the 1981 census, 40.15 per cent of their total population are workers (57.52% males and 20.41% females). As many as 43.30% of the workers are returned to the household industry (which shows their predominant involvement in their traditional occupation). As many as 24.44% are returned as cultivators and 11.43% as agricultural labourers. This is indicative of the changing patterns of their economic life. Only 7.11% are engaged in other than household industries and the remaining 13.72% are engaged in various other services. Child labour exists. Their traditional council at the village level is headed by the Pradhan. At the regional level it is headed by a Chaudhary. Offenders of community norms are made to pay a cash fine or host a punitive feast. The statutory panchayats mainly plan and implement welfare and developmental activities. They are Hindu by faith and their main deities are Bindhya Basini Devi, Biswanath, Ram, Laxmi, Durga, Sati etc. Their village deity is called Dih. Festivals like Ramnavami,

Holi, Diwali, Khichri etc., are celebrated. The ojha performs magical rites for the removal of evil spirits. They have their traditional folk songs and dances which are usually performed at marriages or during festivals. Both males and females participate in singing and dancing.

The Bansphors accept water and food from all the communities except the Dhobi and Nat. Water, the crematorium and village shrines are shared with the other communities. Modern inter-community linkages are forged and developed by businessmen and white-collar workers from amongst them.

Their attitude towards formal education for both boys and girls is negative. Their literacy rate, according to the 1981 census, is only 9.28 (15.48% males and merely 2.24% females). While health and medical facilities are availed of, they still favour indigenous medicare. Their response towards the family planning programme is favourable. Drinking water is available in their localities. A few of them, who have availed of the facilities of the IRDP, are engaged in petty business, poultry farming, etc. The radio, roads, railways, post offices, etc., are the means of communication. Coal, discarded bamboo, split wood, cowdung, etc., are used as domestic fuel. Their attitude towards savings is not positive and they are still dependant on money-lenders and shopkeepers for loans.

Bhangis

They are also known as *Bhangis*, Mehtar, Mehator, Halalkhor and Halalkhor, etc. The term Bhangi has been derived from the Sanskrit word *bhangi* meaning hemp; it seems to be an allusion to their drinking habits. The Bhangi was described as a representative of the Chandala of Manu, who is said to have descended from the union of a Sudra and a Brahmin woman. The Bhangis were traditionally associated with scavenging, sweeping, basket-making etc. In the colonial period they were brought into urban areas to perform the first two roles and became an urban community. With the widespread use of septic latrines and other modes of public convenience, the practice of carrying head-load of nightsoil has perceptibly declined in many parts of urban India. The National Scheme of Liberation and Rehabilitation of Scavengers and their Dependants (1991-92) seeks to liberate them from their existing 'hereditary obnoxious and inhuman occupation of manually removing nightsoil and filth' and to provide for and engage them in 'alternative and dignified occupations' over a period of five years (Annual Report 1991-92, Ministry of Welfare, Government of India, New Delhi). The Bhangis have now taken to other occupations as mentioned below. They are widely distributed in the States of Assam, Maharashtra, Gujarat, Goa and in the Union Territory of Daman & Diu.

They were taken from Bihar, Uttar Pradesh and Orissa to Bengal during the British rule and were engaged as sweepers in municipalities. The Bhangis are notified along with the Hari and Mehtar. Their combined population, according to the 1981 census, is 2,67,465. They speak Hindi and use the Devanagri script. They are bilingual and know Bengali. They are non-vegetarians and their staple cereals are rice and wheat. The two sub-groups among them are the Bhangi and Hela. They have several clans (*gotra*) such as Baghmar, Nagbaisya, Dandal, Parihat, Kanhalya, Birha etc. The clan names are also used as surnames. The Bhangis practise sub-group endogamy and clan exogamy. Vermilion (sindur), bangles and toe-rings are marriage symbols for women. Divorce and remarriage (*churi pahenana*) are allowed. In addition to household chores, their women are engaged in cleaning latrines and lavatories and also in carrying nightsoil from privies. They observe birth pollution for ten days and perform Chhathi on the sixth day. Marriage rituals include worship of the earth (*mager mati*), application of turmeric and oil (*tel-haldi-lepan*), matipujan, marriage bidai, etc. They cremate the dead and observe three days of mourning; after that obsequies (*shradh*) are performed. The traditional and present-day primary occupation of the Bhangis is sweeping roads, cleaning drains and removing nightsoil. Some of them are school teachers and rickshaw-pullers. They have their traditional caste councils known as Shree Sudarshan Seva Samaj at local level and Akhil Bharatiya Sudarshan Samaj at the national level, which looks after their welfare. The Bhangi are Hindu. They especially celebrate the birthday of

Dr. B.R. Ambedkar. They collectively sing devotional songs of Rama. They engage the services of the Brahmins, Napits (barbers), Dhobis (washermen) during life cycle rituals. The level of education is low among the Bhangi. Their literacy rate, along with the Hari and Mehtar, is 15.18% (1981 census). However graduates and post-graduates are found among them. They avail of all the amenities provided by the government.

Dom

Since the late nineteenth century, ethnographers have written about the origin and development of the Doms but the ethnological affinities of the Dom have remained enigmatic. H.H. Elliot considers them to be 'one of the original tribes of India'. The Doms are spread over Punjab, U.P., Bihar, West Bengal, Orissa, Maharashtra and Madhya Pradesh. The Dombara or Domb of Andhra Pradesh, Karnataka and Kerala who are mainly acrobats are substantially different from the Dom. Many and varied legends recounted in different parts of India have attempted only at a rationalisation of their low status and miserable condition. The traditional occupation of Doms includes working in the cremation ground, removing dead cattle, drum beating, scavenging, mat-weaving and basketry. But in recent times they have diversified into various occupations, such as wage labour, animal husbandry and agriculture, a good number of them are engaged as sweepers in various government and private establishments. They share common features of social structure like patrilineal descent and inheritance and patrilocal residence. All of them allow monogamy, junior sororate and levirate, divorce and remarriage.

In Bihar, the Doms are also called Bhangis or Dhangod and claim to be Bansmalik. The Dom are distributed in places like Barh, Mokameh, Bakhtiarpur, Fatuha, Bansghat, Khojkallaghat, Kurjighat and Gulbighat and their habitations are mostly on the banks of the Ganges and around the cremation grounds. In Bihar, they are notified as Dom, Dhangad and their total population, according to the 1981 census, is 2,00,827. The Indo-Aryan language, Magahi, is spoken among themselves and Hindi is spoken with others. The Devanagri script is used. They are non-vegetarians and eat pork, rice and wheat their staple cereals are taken with common pulses like urad, moong and masur along with roots and tubers. Alcoholic drinks are consumed by both the sexes. They are fond of smoking and chewing khaini with betel-leaf.

The four sub-groups amongst them are Praghaiya, Maghaiya or Bansmalik, Bansphor and Ledar. Earlier Dom was used as the surname but now they use Ram, Malik and Prasad. Adult marriage, monogamy, patrilocal residence, predominance of the extended family, junior levirate and sororate are some of their traditional customs. Dowry is prevalent. Paternal property is inherited equally by all the sons and the eldest son succeeds the father. The chhathi-chila is a ritual observed in connection with birth. Marriage rituals are performed at the bride's residence and the marriage feast is hosted by the bride's party. The marriage rituals include sagun, lagan, jhumar, kalsa, chauka, rugsaddi, samdhi, doti and bidai. The dead bodies of adults are cremated and children below the age of five are buried. Death pollution lasts for thirteen days; the dasakarma and kriyakarm or shradh are the mortuary rituals observed. Ancestors are worshipped.

The Dom are landless. Digging graves, cremating dead bodies and making baskets out of bamboo are their traditional occupations. Presently, a good number of them are employed as sweepers and jamadars in the municipal corporations and various other government and private organisations. The secondary occupations pursued are wage labour, rickshaw-pulling, selling charcoal and rearing pigs on a small scale. According to the 1981 census, 39.95% of them are returned as workers (55.30% males and 23.41% females). Of them, 37.37% are engaged in the household industry, *i.e.*, basketry, which is their traditional occupation. This is followed by 28.53% of the workers engaged in agricultural labour and 10.12% as cultivators. The remaining 23.98% of the workers are engaged in various other services including those working in municipal corporations and various government and private organisations as sweepers, jamadars and in other capacities.

The Dom have their own informal council constituted of elderly members for the settlement of disputes. They are Hindus by religion, Ramgosain is a family deity (*Khandani deota*). They worship village deities in addition to gods and goddesses like Kali, Shankerji, Laxmiji, Hanumanji and Krishna Bhagwan. The temple of Kali of Patandevi is their common sacred centre. Babadham or Deoghar, Hariharnath temple at Sonepur and Supanbaba temple in Burdwar are the other sacred centres visited on pilgrimage. Chhat, Dussehra, Hariharnath Mela, Diwali, Holi, Ramnavami, Sawanipujan Rakhibandhan, etc., are the major fairs and festivals celebrated. A Brahmin's services are sought for drawing up horoscopes, for fixing the marriage date and time and for performing death rituals. Tattooing and floor and wall painting are arts associated with them. Basketry is the craft known to them. Folk songs are sung by both men and women. Percussion and wind musical instruments are used. The floors and walls of houses are painted on socio-religious occasions.

Putative kinship relations such as dharabhai are established with most of the neighbouring communities by tying rakhi. In rural areas they are not allowed to share the same well with other communities. They have a separate crematorium located on the fallow land outside the village and it is shared with some specific communities. No restrictions are imposed on them for temple entry.

Their boys and girls generally do not study beyond the primary level. Lack of schooling facilities, poor economic condition and the need to contribute to the family income are the common reasons for them to give up studies. It is evidenced from the census returns that their literacy rate, according to the 1981 census, is only 7.99%. The male and female literacy rates are 13.45% and 2.11% respectively.

Hari

Also known as Hadi or Haddi, they were traditionally engaged in collecting the earthen pots used in burial grounds for death rituals. Apart from West Bengal, they are also returned from Bihar, Uttar Pradesh, Andhra Pradesh, Rajasthan, Maharashtra, Gujarat and

Orissa. They believe that they migrated from Fatehpur in Uttar Pradesh, referred to as Paschima and are now settled in Malda. They are presently distributed in Malda and in West Dinajpur. Risley (1891) is of the opinion that 'the internal structure of the Hari caste throws no light upon its origin, as at the present day, there are no sections and the marriage is regulated solely by counting prohibited degrees'. They are occasional non-vegetarians and eat pork. Rice is their staple cereal. Only their men occasionally take alcoholic drinks. They like to smoke and chew betel-leaf.

All the Hari belong to a single gotra, Aladi, and it has no apparent function. Hierarchical differentiation among the sub-groups prevails at the social level for regulating marriages. Earlier, Harijan and Sardar were used as surnames but at present all of them use Das as their surname. Though the Khom was endogamous group in the past, now it is no longer so. They practise cross-cousin marriages. Adult marriage is common. Marriages are generally settled through negotiation, but marriage by purchase is also in practice. Monogamy is the norm. Conch bangles (*sankha*) and vermilion (*sindur*) are the marriage symbols for women. The earlier practice for bride price payment has given way to dowry payments. After marriage, residence is either neolocal or patrilocal. Both husband and wife can obtain divorce (*char patra*) after it is approved by the community council. Divorce is also secured through law courts. Adultery, barrenness, lack of male child, maladjustment and cruelty are the common grounds on which divorce is secured. Widows, widowers and divorcees can remarry. Both junior levirate and sororate are permissible.

Nuclear and extended families exist. Paternal property is inherited in the ratio of 3:1 by the sons and daughters respectively. The eldest son succeeds to the familial authority. Apart from doing the household chores, women play an important role in social and religious spheres. They contribute to the family income by selling cowdung cakes, basketry, items like tukri-drama and kula, and also earn through midwifery and wage labour. A pre-delivery ritual, sadh, is observed, and birth pollution is practised for seven days after delivery. The post-delivery rituals include mundan, chutir rate, bidhata-bid-huti and annaprasan. On attaining puberty the girl is confined to one part of the household, away from the notice of male members. She is neither allowed into the kitchen nor can she take part in any socio-religious rituals. After about five days she has a bath and is considered pure. Marriage rituals are performed at the bride's house. The fixation of the marriage date (*dindhara*) and an auspicious time (*lagan*), sindurdan, basarghar, bidai, boubhat, astamangala, bari-vasan or madhu-vasan and kapoddhoa are the rituals connected with marriage. The adults are cremated and children below five years are buried. Thirteen days death pollution is observed. There are restrictions on food during the mourning period. A napit's (barber's) services are secured for shaving and a Kantaha Brahmin's services are sought for the observance of the mortuary rite (*shradh*). They also perform ancestor worship.

They are a landless community. Basketry, playing music for others on remuneration, wage labour (*janpait*) and working as midwives (*dai*) are traditional occupations of the Haris.

Lalbegi

Their oral traditions recall that they were earlier Balmiki, but after taking initiation from Saint Kabir have become Lalbegis. They claim that their original home was Rajasthan. The word *Lalbegi* is derived from Lalbeg, the eponymous ancestor of the tribe (Risley, 1891). Their surnames are Begi and Balmiki. They are found in Bihar, U.P., Arunachal Pradesh, Delhi, Meghalaya and Mizoram. They are distributed in Hazaribagh, Ranchi, Jharia, Raniganj, Giridih and Biratnagar.

The Lalbegi of Bihar are also known as Balmiki. Their community name is derived from Lalbeg or Lalguru who is considered a benevolent protector god of the community. They trace their origin to Saint Balmiki. About 200 years back they migrated from Rajasthan to Bihar. They are distributed in the urban areas of Jharia, Dhanbad, Sindri, Katras and Chas in Dhanbad district. Their total population in Bihar, according to the 1981 census, is 932 (489 males and 443 females) and 60.34% of their population are returned from urban areas. The Lalbegi speak in Marwari at home but with outsiders they speak in Hindi. The Devanagri script is used.

The Lalbegis are divided into a number of exogamous gotras such as Bhiwal, Pandit and Chamaria to mention a few. Both adult and child marriages, the latter followed by gaona, are practiced. Monogamy is practised but polygyny is allowed. Junior levirate and junior sororate are permissible. Their women are employed as sweepers and supplement the family income. Child birth, pollution is observed for five days, after which a ceremonial bath (*Nahan*) is given. At the time of marriage the bride and the groom take seven steps (*Satphera*) to the chant of sacred hymns (*Mantras*) in front of the sacred fire (*Havan*). The dead are cremated and death pollution is observed for thirteen days. Death pollution ceases after performing death rites (*Shradh*).

The Lalbegi are a landless community and work as scavengers in municipalities. Some of them are employed as sweepers in the coal-fields and residential houses. According to the 1981 census, 31.87% of them are returned as workers (46.63% males and 15.58% females). Out of them a majority *i.e.*, 53.87% are returned under other services which refers to their major involvement in their traditional occupation of scavenging. However, a good number of them are also returned as agricultural labourers (30.64%) and a small number (6.73%) of workers are returned as cultivators. The remaining 8.76% of the workers are engaged in other services.

They are Hindu by faith. The Lalbegi organised an inter-state socio-religious movement for their social upliftment under the banner of Bihar-Bengal Balmiki Panchayat.

As an untouchable community, tradtionally engaged in sweeping, scavenging etc., they have very little interaction with other communities at the ritual and social levels. Other Harijan communities like the Hadi, Dom, Mela, Musahar etc., accept water and food from them.

Their literacy rate according to the 1981 census is 18.24%. Their males have made satisfactory progress in the field of education and their literacy rate is 30.06%. They make use of both modern and traditional medicare and show a positive attitude towards family planning. Some of them are self-employed and rear pigs. The facilities of mass media communication and the public distribution system are being availed of.

Mehtars

The term Mehtar, meaning a prince or leader, is an ironic title given to the people who are traditionally engaged as sweepers and scavengers and are known by different names in different parts of the country like Bhangi, Hari, Lalbegi and so on. The Mehtars, who are the followers of the patron saint Lalbeg, are called Lalbegi. By faith they are either Muslim or Hindu. Russell and Hiralal (1916) note that 'the Shaikh Mehtars are the only real Muhammadan branch, for though the Lalbegi worship a Musalman Saint they remain Hindu'.

The Mehtar in Bihar are also known as *Hari* and *Bhangi*. The Bengali name Hari is supposed to have come from haddi, meaning bone, and is thus a bone-gatherer. The term Bhangi is derived from the Sanskrit bhanga (hemp), a narcotic drug used as an intoxicant. The Mehtars are found all over the state and their total population in Bihar is 1,56,349 (returned as Hari, Mehtar, Bhangi) according to the 1981 census. Of them, 36.85% are returned from urban areas. They speak in the Indo-Aryan language Angika and Hindi is spoken with others. The script used is Devanagri. They are non-vegetarian and eat pork; their staple food consists of rice, wheat and pulses like arhar, urad, moong and masur. Men regularly take alcoholic drinks whereas, women occasionally take liquor. They smoke beedis, cigarettes and hemp (*Cannabis sativa*) and chew tobacco (khaini) and betel-leaf very frequently.

The Mehtar are divided into thirteen sub-divisions, namely, Chaparia, Dom, Dhapra, Ladhora, Amdaria, Koelbari, Sariswar, Khavis, Mochi, Mushahar, Dusadh or Dosad, Bansphor and Mouli. They belong to the Kashyap gotra. In the district of East Champaran they have five sub-divisions which are not there in Purnea district. These sub-divisions are Amdaria, Koelbari, Machua, Manhji and Sariswar. The marriageable age for girls and boys is eighteen and twenty-five years, respectively. Negotiated marriage (Pancheri cheka) is the usual mode. Monogamy is the rule but many cases of non-sororal polygyny are also reported. Vermilion is the symbol of marriage for women. Dowry is given in cash and kind. They are patrilocal in residence and partilineal in descent. Divorce is permitted with social approval. The remarriage (*Chumanna* or *Dowa*) of widows and divorcees is permitted but no rituals or ceremonies are observed. They mostly live in either nuclear or extended families though of late, the former arc on the increase. Only sons inherit property. The eldest son succeeds the father. Their women contribute to family income by working as scavengers in municipalities, district boards and hospitals. The women's role in the religious festivals, marriages and birth rites is quite prominent. On the sixth day after birth *chhathi* ceremony is observed in which all the women and children of the hamlet participate and partake of sweets after the barber tonsures the newborn child and pares the mother's nails to complete the birth pollution period. The tonsure (*Mundan*) ceremony is observed only for boys between five and seven years. Marriages are solemnised at the bride's house and the marriage feast is hosted for the bridegroom's party along with the friends and relatives of the bride. The second feast is given by the bridegroom's party on the day after the groom reaches his house along with the bride. The marriage ceremony consists of rituals such as ganabajan varagamah pair dhualai, parchawan, saptapadi, sindurdan and bidai. The marriage is consummated at the bridegroom's house. The dead are either buried or cremated.

The Mehtar are engaged in multifarious occupations such as sweeping and removing garbage in municipal and notified areas, bamboo, basketry, scavenging and playing drums (*Dhols*) during marriages and festivals. Their women act as midwives. According to the 1981 census, out of their total population 32.49% are workers (48.96% males and 15.00% females). Of them 37.85% workers are returned under other services which refers to the Mehtars engaged in their traditional occupation. However, 40.12% of the workers are returned as agricultural labourers and only 6.26% are returned as cultivators. Only 8.28% of the workers are engaged in manufacturing, processing etc., which probably refers to basketry.

The remaining 7.49% of the workers are engaged in other services. Some of them work as agricultural labourers and casual labourers on a daily wage basis.

Inter-community disputes are settled by the elders of the hamlet or are referred to the statutory panchayat. They profess Hinduism and worship different gods and goddesses. Their family deities are Kali and Durga. The village deities are Gangamai and Mahavirji. The important traditional festivals they celebrate are Chhat, Durgapuja, Holi, Diwali and Ramnavami. They also observe Saint Ravi Das Jayanti and Baba Ambedkar Jayanti. They engage sacred specialists from the Brahmin community, but in the absence of a Brahmin they engage a priest (gossain) belonging to the community of mendicants, who worship and officiate at birth, marriage and death rites.

Traditional inter-community linkages exist with some neighbouring communities like Dusadh and Dom. They accept water, and kacha or pucca food from all the other communities, but other communities neither accept kacha nor pucca food from them nor do they share water sources and crematoria with Mehtars. They participate in traditional festivals but have no special role.

Mishra (1978) refers to a study of the Darbhanga Mehtars to highlight the role of the Mehtar caste Panchayat and its role in social reform measures like enforcing adult marriage, prohibiting dowry and several other rules in order to reduce expenses as well as to bring in a modicum of uniformity in the practices within the community.

Their literacy rate according to the 1981 census is 16.42% (26.50% males and 5.72% females). Though they have a favourable attitude towards modern medicare, only a few can afford it. They use indigenous medicines for common diseases. Their attitude towards the family planning programme is favourable. The midday meal scheme for children and ration shops are made use of but banking facilities are not used. They are still dependent on moneylenders.

ANNEXURE—B

OCCUPATIONAL MOBILITY AMONG THE SCAVENGERS OF PATNA

The Sulabh International Social Service Organisation conducted a rapid survey of 1,038 scavenger households in Patna in 1996. Some interesting findings in the form of tables are given below. This depicts the housing situation, the size of households, the income levels of the households and the occupational diversity in the scavenger households. It is clear that the bulk of the scavengers are still working as sweepers. However, many scavengers are employed as mechanic, compounder, clerk, peon, rikshaw-puller, daily wage earner etc. The figures also reveal that over 60% of the scavengers are literate and some have even become graduate.

Socio-economic Status and Occupational Mobility of Scavengers in Patna

A. *Housing Situation*

Table 1: Own house

(N = 1038)

1.	Yes	21.39%
	No	63.43%
	No Response	16.18%
	Total	100%

Table 2 : If not having own house

1.	Rented Room	5.39%
2.	Hut	41.33%
3.	Rented Hut	1.06%
4.	Pucca Room (Rented)	3.37%
5.	Kacha Room Rented	5.39%
6.	Govt. Quarter	31.70%
7.	No Response	11.37%
	Total	100%

Table 3: Size of the Households

1.	Less than 5	58.44%
2.	5 to 10	40.80%
3.	10+	0.76%
	Total	100%

Table 4: Household Income

1.	Up to Rs. 1000	25.00%
2.	Rs. 1001 to 2000	56.08%
3.	Rs. 2001 to 4000	15.06%
4.	Rs. 4000 +	3.86%
	Total	100%

Table 5: Occupationwise Distribution

1.	Sweeper	66.18%
2.	Mechanic	0.48%
3.	Compounder	0.67%
4.	Tailor	0.29%
5.	Clerk	0.67%
6.	Peon	2.79%
7.	Pensioner	4.24%
8.	Dresser	0.10%
9.	Private Sweeper	1.16%
10.	Rickshaw-Puller	0.29%
11.	Fitter	0.67%
12.	Labourer	2.22%
13.	Housewife	2.73%
14.	Unemployed	2.00%
15.	Others	14.64%

Table 6: State of Education

(N = 1038)

1.	Illiterate	38.59%
2.	Literate	6.66%
3.	Non-Matric	47.99%
4.	Matric	6.07%
5.	Graduate	1.18%

ANNEXURE—C

LIST OF TOP ACHIEVERS

1. ***Shri Bhola Ram Tufani***—Shri Tufani was a former Minister of Animal Husbandry, Government of Bihar. He represented the Shikarpur (SC) Constituency in West Champaran.
2. ***Shri Girija Shankar Prasad***—Shri Prasad is an inhabitant of Ambedkar Colony, Sandalpur, Patna. He is M.A. in Sociology and History, M.B.A. and LL.B. At present he is an Advocate in Patna High Court. He is the convener of the Dalit Cell of Lok Paksha and associated with Bihar Rajya Raut Mehtar Panchayat. His father the late Ganpat Ram was the President of Hind Sweeper Sevak Samaj (Bihar Branch) founded by Pandit Govind Ballabh Pant. Both his parents worked as sweepers. His mother was working as a scavenger in private houses. Being a member of scavenger family Mr. Girija Shankar has suffered indignities a number of times at the hands of upper caste persons. He has been associated with Sulabh International Social Services Organisation at New Delhi for some years. At present he is the Secretary of Ambedkar Suraksha Manch.
3. ***Dr. Mohan Ram***—Dr. Mohan Ram is an M.L.A. from Darbhanga (Rural) Constituency. He is a teacher in a college.
4. ***Shri Pritam Hari***—He is the son of Shri Jagdish Hari who was Sanitary Inspector in Bhagalpur Municipality. Now Pritam Hari is in the Bihar Administrative Service. Currently he is an Additional District Magistrate.
5. ***Smt. Leela Devi***—She is the Secretary of Purnea Municipality Employees Union. She is a highly influential lady although she is only non-Matric. She is a good orator. She advances loans to needy scavengers in Purnea.

6. ***Arun Kumar Ram***—Shri A.K. Ram is an inhabitant of Darbhanga. He is a social worker and associated with Bharatiya Janata Party. He graduated with Botany Honours. His wife is also I.Sc. He has keen interest in education. He wants to contribute to the educational development of the Dalits and other Backward Communities.
7. ***Rajendra Ram***—Rajendra Ram is M.A. in Political Science. He is a member of monitoring committee of Scheduled Caste Development Corporation.
8. ***Ram Babu Prasad***—Shri Ram Babu Prasad is resident of Mithapur B Area. He is a graduate. He is associated with many social organisations from his student life. He is National Vice-chairman of Ambedkar Suraksha Manch. He has been Mukhiya of Bihar Rajya Raut Mehtar Panchayat. It is a caste Panchayat. He is the Founder General Secretary of Akhil Bharatiya Mehtar Mahasabha and Secretary of Harijan Utthan Parishad and Safai Mazdoor Maha Sangh. He was General Secretary, Harijan Evam Adivasi Cell of Bihar Pradesh Congress Committee. He is also the General Secretary of Naya Bharat Party. He has been inspired by Dr. Ambedkar's principle : educate, organise and agitate. His mission is to enforce prohibition among the scavengers and to work for education of boys and girls. He dislikes serving meat and liquor at the time of marriage or Shradh. He is keen to provide employment to educated youth through a special programme by the government.
9. ***Shri Sajawal Raut***—He is a Sanitary Inspector in Patna Medical College and Hospital. He is a good social worker. Late Bhola Raut a former long-term Congress M.P. adopted him. He is a Vice-chairman of Ambedkar Suraksha Manch and Akhil Bharatiya Mehtar Sabha. He is associated with Trade Unions. Due to his efforts a statue of Dr. Bhimrao Ambedkar has been installed in P.M.C.H., Patna.
10. ***Dr. Munna***—He is a Doctor in Indira Gandhi Institute of Cardiology, Patna. He is a son of a scavenger. His father is not alive. His mother is still serving as a sweeper in P.M.C.H., Patna.

11. ***Smt. Neelam Devi***—She is Principal, Ambedkar Institute of Research and Rehabilitation, Patna. She is a good singer. She is trained in typing and shorthand. She has passed B.A. She is associated with Sulabh International since 1987. Her grandmother had worked as a scavenger. Her husband Shri Anand Prasad is an Assistant in the secretariat.
12. ***Shri Tufani Ram***—He is an active Safai Mazdoor Union leader. He is a veteran Union leader and associated with many organisations. He is General Secretary of Harijan Utthan Parishad and Cooperative Employees Union and President of State Dalit Cell of Rashtriya Janata Dal and Bihar State Safai Karmi Mazdoor Union.

    He has been agitating against corruption, ill-treatment of scavengers and nepotism rampant in the Corporation administration. He has used his influence to get some Indira Awas houses for the scavengers.

BIBLIOGRAPHY

Chatterjee, M.S. (1981), *Reversible Sex Roles: The Special Case of Benaras Sweepers*, Pergamon Press, Oxford, England.

Dumont, L. (1970), *Homo Hierarchicans*, University of Chicago Press, Chicago.

Fuchs, Stephen (1981), *At the Bottom of Indian Society*, Munshiram Manoharlal Publishers Pvt. Ltd., New Delhi.

Karlekar, Malavika (1976), *A Study of Balmiki Women in Delhi*, Oxford University Press, Delhi.

Pandya, B.V. (1959), *Striving for Economic Equality*, Popular Prakashan, Bombay.

Pathak, B. (1994), *Road to Freedom*, Motilal Banarsidas Publishers Pvt. Ltd., New Delhi.

Pathak, B. (ed.) 1998), *Continuity and Change in Indian Society*, Concept Publishing Company, New Delhi.

Sharma, R. (1995), *Scavengers in Indian Society*, M.B. Publications Pvt. Ltd., New Delhi.

Sinha, B.D., Menon, P.S.K. and Ghosh, A.K. (1994), *Restoration of Human Dignity*, Arnold Publishers, New Delhi.

Srivastava, B.N. (1997), Manual Scavenging in India: A Disgrace to the Country, Concept Publishing Company, New Delhi.

ARTICLES

Saberwal, Satish (1973), Receding Pollution: Inter-caste Relations in Urban Punjab, *Sociological Bulletin*, Vol. 122, No. 2.

Sachchidananda (1994), Inequality in India: Sociological Perspectives, *IASSI Quarterly*, New Delhi, Vol. 3, No. 1&2.

Shyam Lal (1981), *Caste and Political Mobilisation: The Bhangis*, Panchsheel Prakashan, Jaipur.

Shyam Lal (1990), Origin of Bhangi: A Hypothesis, *The Eastern Anthropologist*, 44:2.

Shyam Lal (1992), *The Bhangi—A Sweeper Caste, Its Socio-Economic Portraits*, Popular Prakashan, Bombay.

Shyam Lal (1973), Sanskritisation and Social Change among Bhangis in Jodhpur, *Indian Journal of Social Work*, No. 34.

Kiang, S. (1974), Plight of Women Sweepers, *Mainstream*, Vol. 12, No. 50.

Gangrade, K.D. (1975), Social Mobility in India: A Study of Depressed Classes, *Man India*, Vol. 54, No. 3.

REPORTS

Kaka Kalelkar (1955), "Backward Classes Commission", Govt. of India, New Delhi.

Barve, V.N. (1958), Report of the Scavengers' Living Condition Enquiry Committee, State of Bombay, Director, Government Printing, Publication and Stationery, Bombay State, Bombay.

Malkani, N.R. (1961), Report of Scavenging Conditions Enquiry Committee, Ministry of Home Affairs, Government of India, New Delhi.

Malkani, N.R. (1966), Report of the Committee on Customary Rights to Scavenging, Ministry of Home Affairs, Government of India, New Delhi.

Report of the Commission for Scheduled Castes and Scheduled Tribes, Ministry of Home Affairs, Government of India, New Delhi.

Roy Burman, B.K. (1961), Study of Customary Rights and Living and Working Conditions of Scavengers in Two Towns, Census of India, Monograph Series Vol. 1, Part XI, Office of Registrar, Ministry of Home Affairs, Government of India, New Delhi.

Seminar Report (1992), National Seminar on Action Sociology and Liberation of Scavenger, Indian Association of Action Sociologists and Sulabh International, New Delhi.

INDEX